STUDIES IN BIBLE DOCTRINE

By
J. Paul Reno
Pastor and Author

Published by
Blessed Hope Publishers
Hagerstown, Md.

All Scripture quotations in this book are taken from the
King James Version of the Bible.

Formatting and publishing assisted by:
The Old Paths Publications, Inc.
www.theoldpathspublications.com
TOP@theoldpathspublications.com

Disclaimer

The author of this work has quoted the writers of many articles and books. This does not mean that the author endorses or recommends the works of others. If the author quotes someone, it does not mean that he agrees with all of the author's tenets, statements, concepts, or words, whether in the work quoted or any other work of the author. There has been no attempt to alter the meaning of the quotes; and therefore, some of the quotes are long in order to give the entire sense of the passage.

Copyright © 2014 by J. Paul Reno
All Rights Reserved
Printed in the United States of America

ISBN 978-0-9860377-6-4

All Scripture quotes are from the King James Bible

No part of this work may be reproduced without the expressed consent of the publisher, except for brief quotes, whether by electronic, photocopying, recording, or information storage and retrieval systems.

Address All Inquiries To:
THE OLD PATHS PUBLICATIONS, Inc.
142 Gold Flume Way
Cleveland, Georgia, U.S.A. 30528

Web: www.theoldpathspublications.com
E-mail: TOP@theoldpathspublications.com

1.0

DEDICATION

My dear wife who has prayed for me and assisted me in HIS work for nearly 50 years. Also I dedicate this to my five children who are serving our Lord in full time gospel work.

Pastor J. Paul Reno

PREFACE

The following notes have been developed over a period of 45 plus years of pastoring. They are the result of 60 years as a Christian and reading my Bible, learning from over 80 Bible teachers, and teaching common people. They will bear similarities to others and their writings. I have benefited from their labors. I greatly appreciate what has been done and wish I had the eyesight and time to retrace my studies and give credit where it is due.

May God get praise and glory from what proves helpful. I take responsibility for that which is in error. May we all aim to follow the motto, "The Bible, the whole Bible and nothing but the Bible."

Pastor J. Paul Reno

TABLE OF CONTENTS

Contents

STUDIES IN BIBLE DOCTRINE 1
DEDICATION 3
PREFACE 5
TABLE OF CONTENTS 7
CHAPTER 1: THE SCRIPTURES 55
    II Tim. 3:15-17 55
   Five purposes of Scriptures 55
  II Pet. 1:16-21 56
  I Pet. 1:9-12 56
  I Thess. 2:13 56
  Matt. 22:29 56
  II Pet. 3:15, 16 – Wrong attitude or use of Scriptures brings destruction 56
  Rev. 22:18, 19 56
  Matt. 15:1-6 57
  Luke 16:29-31 57
  Luke 24:25-27 57
  Luke 24:44-49 57
  John 5:39, 45-47 57
  I Cor. 2:9-14 57
  Heb. 1:1-3 57
  Consider the Bible: 58
  Amos 8:11, 12 58
  Jer. 23:30 58
  II Cor. 2:17 58
  I Pet. 1:23, 25 58
  Matt. 7:15-20 59

Psm. 119:89 59
Psm. 119:160 59
Psm. 138:2 59
Matt. 5:18 59
Mark 13:31 (also Luke 21:33) 60
Luke 16:17 60
John 10:35b 60
John 17:17 60
Psm. 119:140 60
Psm. 12:6, 7 60

Consider the versions: 60
Eph. 6:17 61
Psm. 119:9 61
Psm. 119:11 61
Psm. 119:63 61
Psm. 119:72 61
Psm. 119:105 61
Psm. 119:126 61
Psm. 119:126 62

RULES OF BIBLE INTERPRETATION 62
II Tim. 2:15 62
Mark 7:9, 13 62
Jer. 23:36 62
II Cor. 4:2 62
Heb. 4:2 62
II Pet. 3:16 63
I Tim. 6:20 63
I Pet. 1:11 63
I I Pet. 1:20 63
James 1:22 63

TABLE OF CONTENTS

    Luke 24:25 64
    Eph. 6:17 64
    Rev. 1:20 64
    Mark 4:1-20 64
    Daniel 8:1-27 64
    Gal. 4:22-31 64
    John 5:46, 47 65
WAYS TO LEARN FROM THE BIBLE **65**
CONSIDER YOUR DESIRES AND ATTITUDES: **65**
    I Pet. 2:2 65
    Rom. 15:4 66
    Psm. 119:10 66
    Psm. 119:103 66
    I Thess. 4:11 66
WE MUST TAKE TIME TO HEAR FROM GOD: **66**
    Psm. 119:147, 148 66
WE SHOULD HAVE A PLAN: **66**
    Psm. 119:18, 27, 28 66
    Psm. 119:15 66
    Psm. 119:11 67
    Psm. 119:7 67
LET GOD THE HOLY SPIRIT TEACH YOU: **67**
    John 14:26 67
    I John 2:27 68
CHAPTER 2: WHO IS GOD? **69**
    GOD 69
    I Cor. 2:9-16 69
    Heb. 11:5, 6 69
    Rom. 10:17 69
    Rom. 1:18-32 69

Psm. 14:1-3	70
Gen. 1:1	70
John 17:3	70

ETERNAL **70**

Gen. 21:33	70
Ex. 3:13, 14	70
Deut. 33:27	70
Psm. 90:2	70
Psm. 102:24-27	71
Heb. 1:10-12	71
Isa. 44:6	71
Isa. 57:15	71

GOD IS SPIRIT **71**

John 4:23, 24	71
Luke 24:39	72
John 1:18	72
John 14:7-10	72

GOD HAS ALL KNOWLEDGE (OMNISCIENCE) **72**

Rom. 11:32-36	72
I John 3:20	72
Psm. 147:4, 5	72
Psm. 139:1-4	72
Prov. 15:3	73
Acts 15:18	73

GOD NEVER CHANGES (IMMUTABILITY) **73**

Mal. 3:6	73
James 1:17	73
Num. 23:19	73
Heb. 6:13-20	73
Heb. 13:8	73

TABLE OF CONTENTS

    Jonah 3:9, 10 73

    Gen. 6:5-7 74

EXAMPLE **74**

GOD HAS ALL POWER (OMNIPOTENCE) **74**

    Matt. 19:16-26 74

    Jer. 32:27, 17 74

    Gen. 17:1 74

    Job 42:1, 2 75

    Dan. 4:35 75

    Rev. 19:6 75

    EXAMPLES OF HIS POWER: 75

GOD IS ALL PRESENT (OMNIPRESENT) **75**

    Main residence in heaven, but spirit being everywhere 75

    Psm. 139:7-11 75

    I Kings 8:27 75

    Jer. 23:23, 24 76

    Matt. 18:20 76

    John 14:23 76

    Acts 17:24-28 76

    John 20:17 76

    Results: 76

GOD IS HOLY **76**

    I Pet. 1:16 76

    Isa. 6:3-7 76

    Rev. 4:8 77

    Heb. 12:14 77

    Lev. 11:43-45 77

    I John 1:5 77

    Psm. 99:9 77

    John 17:11 77

Acts 3:14	77
Eph. 4:13	77
Rom. 1:4	78
Hab. 1:12, 13	78

GOD IS A TRINITY 78
- I John 5:7 78
- I Cor. 13:12 78
- Matt. 28:19, 20 79

UNITY 79
- Deut. 6:4, 5 79
- Isa. 44:6 79
- John 10:27-33 80
- I Tim. 2:5 80
- Mark 10:17, 18 80

THREE IN ONE 80
- Gen. 1:26, 27 80
- Gen. 3:22 80
- Gen. 11:6, 7 80
- Psm. 2:7, 12 80
- Isa. 7:14 80
- Isa. 9:6, 7 81
- Isa. 6:8 81
- Isa. 48:16 81
- Matt. 3:16, 17 81
- John 14:16-36 81
- II Cor. 13:14 81

CHAPTER 3: GOD THE FATHER 83
- SEPARATE PERSONHOOD AND TITLE 83
- Matt. 28:19 83
- I John 5:7 83

TABLE OF CONTENTS

John 14:16, 26 83
Titus 3:3-6 83
I Cor. 15:24 83
Eph. 2:13-18 83
I John 2:1 83
I John 2:22, 23 83
Mark 1:10, 11 84
Acts 10:38 84

FATHER OF THE SECOND MEMBER OF THE TRINITY 84
John 8:28, 29 84
John 17:1-5 84
Hebrews 1:1-2 84
Hebrews 1:5-9 84
II Cor. 1:3, 4 84
Gal. 4:4 85
John 3:16 85
Matt. 8:29 85
Eph. 1:3, 4 85
Col. 1:19 85

FATHER (SPIRITUAL) OF THE SAVED 85
Matt. 23:9 85
John 1:12, 13 85
Rom. 8:15-17 85
I Pet. 1:3-5 85
II Pet. 1:2-4 86
John 20:17 86
I John 1:3 86
I John 3:1-3 86
II Cor. 6:17, 18 86
Contrast: John 8:44 86

- Matt. 13:38 86
- Eph. 2:2, 3 86

CREATOR 87
- (MENTIONED OVER 100 TIMES IN SCRIPTURE) 87
- Gen. 1:1 87
- Neh. 9:6 87

UNSEEN 87
- Col. 1:15 87
- John 1:18 87
- John 14:7-9 87

INVOLVED IN OUR SALVATION 87
- John 3:16 87
- Gal. 4:4, 5 87
- Isa. 53:6, 10, 11 88
- Col. 1:12-14 88
- Heb. 9:14 88

HAS A WILL 88
- Eph. 1:11 88
- Isa. 14:26, 27 88
- Isa. 46:9-11 88
- Dan. 4:35 89
- Rom. 8:28-31 89
- John 6:37 89
- II Thess. 2:13, 14 89

CHAPTER 4: GOD THE SON 91
- THE LORD JESUS CHRIST 91
- LORD 91
- Rom. 14:9 91
- I Cor. 12:3 91
- Matt. 26:21-25 91

TABLE OF CONTENTS

    Matt. 7:21-23 91
    Isa. 43:11 92
    Isa. 33:22 92
JESUS 92
    Matt. 1:21 93
    John 14:13-15 93
CHRIST 93
    Matt. 24: 4, 5 93
    John 1:20, 25 93
    John 4:24-26 93
    Matt. 16:16, 17 94
    PRE-EXISTENCE 94
    Micah 5:2 94
    Isa. 9:6 94
    John 1:1-4 94
    John 1:14, 15 94
    John 8:56-59 94
    John 17:5 95
    Phil. 2:5-11 95
    Col. 1:15-19 95
    Rev. 1:8 95
DEITY 95
DIVINITY 95
Deity 95
IMPORTANCE 96
    John 1:12 96
    I Cor. 15:17-19 96
HIS CLAIMS 96
    Luke 22:66-23:2 96
    John 10:30-33 96

John 10:36-39	96
John 14:7-11	96
BIBLE TEACHING	96
Matt. 16:16, 17	96
Matt. 28:18-20	97
Mark 2:5-11	97
John 1:1-3	97
John 17:1-3	97
John 20:27-29	97
Acts 3:12-15	97
Acts 7:57-60	97
Rom. 9:1-5	98
II Cor. 13:14	98
Col. 1:13-19	98
Col. 2:8, 9	98
I Tim. 2:3-5	98
I Tim. 6:14-16	98
II Tim. 4:1	98
Titus 2:13	98
Heb. 1:1-10	99
Rev. 1:17, 18	99
Rev. 1:17:18 –	99
Isa. 44:6 –	99
Isa. 48:11, 12 –	99
Isa. 41:4 –	99
Rev.22:12-15 –	99
Rev. 1:8 –	100
INCARNATION	100
Gen. 3:14, 15	100
Gal. 3:16	100

TABLE OF CONTENTS

Gen. 21:12 –	100
Gen. 49:10 –	100
Acts 2:29, 30	100
Psm. 69:7-9	101
Isa. 7:14	101
Isa. 9:6	101
Matt. 1:18-23	101
Luke 1:26-35, 46, 47	101
John 1:14	101
John 3:13	102
John 8:41	102
Gal. 4:4, 5	102
Phil. 2:6, 7, 8	102
Col. 4:14	102
I Tim. 3:16	102
Heb. 2:9	102
Heb. 2:14	103
Heb. 2:16-18	103
I John 4:1-3	103
THE SINLESS LIFE OF JESUS	103
Isa. 53:9	103
I Pet. 2:22	103
Matt. 27:3, 4	103
Matt. 27:19	103
Mark 1:23, 24	103
Luke 9:29	103
Luke 23:41, 27	104
John 1:4, 5	104
John 3:19-21	104
John 8:12	104

John 8:46	104
John 14:30	104
John 18:38	104
John 19:4-6	104
Acts 3:14	104
Acts 4:27, 28	105
II Cor. 5:20, 21	105
Heb. 1:8, 9	105
Heb. 5:9	105
Heb. 7:26-28	105
I Pet. 1:19	105
I Pet. 2:21-24	105
I Pet. 3:18	106
I John 1:5	106
I John 3:3	106
I John 3:5	106
SUBSTITUTIONARY DEATH	106
Gen. 2:17	106
Gen. 3:21	106
Gen. 4:1-5	106
Gen. 22:7, 8	106
Exodus 11	107
Leviticus	107
Psm. 22:1, 7, 8	107
Psm. 22:14-18	107
Psm. 69:7-9	107
Isa. 52:13; 53:12	107
Zech. 13:6	107
Matt. 16:21-23	107
Luke 24:25-27	108

TABLE OF CONTENTS

John 10:11 108
John 10:17, 18 108
John 12:23, 24 108
John 12:31-33 108
I Cor. 2:8 108
Acts 2:22-24 109
Rom. 4:24, 25 109
Rom. 5:6-8 109
Rom. 8:31, 32 109
I Cor. 5:7 109
I Cor. 6:20 109
I Cor.15:3, 4 109
Gal. 3:13, 14 110
Heb. 2:9, 14-18 110
Heb. 9:25-28 110
I Pet. 1:10-12 110
I Pet. 1:18-20 110
I Pet. 2:24 110
I Pet. 3:18 110
I John 2:2 110
Rev. 5:8-12 111
Rev. 13:8 111
JESUS' BLOOD – THE WORK IT DOES 111
Acts 20:28 111
Rom. 5:8, 9 111
I Cor. 10:16 111
Eph. 1:7 111
Eph. 2:8-13 112
Col. 1:20 112
Heb. 9:12 112

Heb. 9:14	112
Heb. 10:19	112
Heb. 13:12	112
Heb. 13:20	112
I Pet. 1:2	113
I John 1:7	113
I John 5:8	113
Rev. 5:9	113
Rev. 12:11	113
Acts 5:28	113
Heb. 10:29	113
Rom. 3:25	114
Heb. 12:24	114
Rev. 7:14	114
Matt. 27:4 – Teaches that Jesus' blood was "*innocent blood*." No guilt could there be found. In this, it is different from any human blood.	114
Acts 20:28 and I John 1:7	114
I Pet. 1:19	114
JESUS' BURIAL	114
I Cor. 15:1-4	115
Rom. 6:1-6	115
Matt. 12:38-40	115
Eph. 4:7-11	115
Luke 16:19-26	115
Col. 2:14, 15	116
Col. 2:12, 13	116
Heb. 2:14, 15	116
Gen. 22:8	116
Acts 2:25-31	116
Luke 23:43	117

TABLE OF CONTENTS

I Pet. 3:18-20 117
Heb. 9:12, 23-28 117
– John 20:17, 18 – Jesus asked not to be touched as He hadn't yet ascended. 117
– Matt. 28:9 – A short time later Jesus allowed Himself to be touched and held. 117
– John 20:27 – Jesus now invites Thomas to touch Him. 117
Mark 14:3-9 117
Luke 23:46 118
JESUS' RESURRECTION 118
I Cor. 15:1-4 119
I Cor. 15:5-8 119
Acts 1:1-3 119
John 20:14-20 119
John 20:26-29 119
John 21:1, 9-14 119
Luke 24:13-16, 30 119
Luke 24:36-45 120
Acts 1:3-11 120
Acts 2:22-24 120
Acts 20:7 120
Rev. 1:18 120
Matt. 28:5, 6 120
Luke 24:12 120
John 20:9 121
I Cor. 15:12-19 121
I Cor. 15:20-23 121
RESULTS OF JESUS' RESURRECTION 121
Acts 13:26-38 121
Acts 17:30-32 121
Rom. 1:4 121
Rom. 7:4 121

Rom. 14:9	121
I Cor. 15:22	121
II Cor. 4:14	121
Eph. 1:19, 20	122
Col. 3:1	122
Heb. 7:25	122
I Pet. 1:3, 4	122
Rev. 1:18	122
Acts 20:7 etc.	122
John 16:7 (20:22 and Acts 2)	122
ASCENSION OF CHRIST	122
Mark 16:19, 20	122
Luke 24:49-53	122
Acts 7:54-59	122
JESUS' PRESENT MINISTRY	123
John 14:16	123
John 14:20	123
Matt. 16:18	123
Rom. 8:34	123
Eph. 1:22, 23	123
Eph. 4:7-11	123
Eph. 5:25-27	123
I Tim. 2:5	124
Heb. 2:18	124
Heb. 2:17	124
I Pet. 2:25	124
I John 1:3-7	124
I John 2:1	124
Jude 1	124
Rev. 4:11	124

TABLE OF CONTENTS

CHAPTER 5: GOD THE HOLY SPIRIT 125
    PERSONALITY – HE IS A PERSON 125
    PERSONAL TRAITS 125
    I Cor. 2:10 125
    I Cor. 2:11 125
    I Cor. 12:11 125
    Rom. 15:30 125
    Rom. 8:27 125
    PERSONAL ACTIONS 125
    I Tim. 4:1 125
    Rev. 2:7 125
    Luke 12:12 126
    John 14:26 126
    Acts 13:2 126
    Rom. 8:26 126
    Rom. 8:14 126
    RECEIVES PERSONAL TREATMENT 126
    Matt. 12:31, 32 126
    Acts 5:3 126
    Acts 5:9 126
    Acts 7:51 126
    Heb. 10:29 126
    Eph. 4:30 127
    ASSOCIATED WITH THE OTHER TWO PERSONS OF THE GODHEAD 127
    Matt. 28:19 127
    II Cor. 13:14 127
    I John 5:7 127
    PERSONAL CHARACTERS AND OFFICES 127
    John 14:26 127
    John 14:16 128

John 14:26	128
John 16:7	128
HIS DEITY – THE HOLY SPIRIT IS GOD!	128
HE IS CALLED GOD.	128
II Cor. 3:17, 18	128
Acts 5:3, 4	128
I Cor. 3:16, 17	128
I Cor. 12:4-6	128
HE HAS DIVINE ATTRIBUTES.	128
Rom. 1:4	128
Heb. 9:14	128
Psm. 139:7-10	129
Luke 1:35	129
I Cor. 2:10-11	129
HE HAS DONE WORKS.	129
Job 26:13; 33:4	129
II Pet. 1:21	129
Matt. 1:20	129
Matt. 12:28	129
Acts 13:2-4	130
Acts 20:28	130
I Cor. 12:11	130
HIS MINISTRY(S)	130
Gen. 1:2	130
Gen. 6:3	130
John 16:7-11	130
II Thess. 2:5-7	130
John 3:3-8	130
Rom. 8:9	131
II Cor. 1:22	131

TABLE OF CONTENTS

- Rom. 8:14 131
- Rom. 8:16 131
- Acts 1:8 131
- John 14:26 131
- Eph. 3:16 132
- Rom. 8:2 132
- Jude 20 132
- Phil. 3:3 132
- John 16:14 132
- Gal. 5:22, 23 132
- Rom. 8:11, 23 132
- Rom. 8:1-27 132
- Rom. 10:17 133
- I Cor. 6:11 133
- I John 2:27, 20 133
- II Cor. 13:14 133
- BAPTISM(S) 133
- Baptism by the Spirit 133
  - I Cor. 12:12, 13 - 133
- Baptism with the Holy Ghost 133
  - John 1:32-24 - 133
- FILLING(S) 134
  - Eph. 5:18 134
  - Eph. 5:19-6:18 134
  - Acts 2:1-12 134
  - Acts 4:8, 13 135
  - Acts 4:29-31 135
  - Acts 6:1-7 135
  - Acts 9:17 135
  - Acts 11:22-24 135

- Acts 13:6-12 135
- Acts 13:50-52 135
- Luke 4:1-2 135
- Luke 1:15 136
- Eph. 5:18 136
- John 7:37-39 136
- Col. 3:15-16 136
- Gal. 5:16-24 136
- Eph. 4:22-24 136
- Luke 11:13 136
- Mark 11:24 136

Three important questions: 137
- HIS LEADING 137
- Jer. 10:23 137
- Isa. 63:10-14 137

ILLUSTRATIONS: 137
- Acts 8:27-29 137
- Acts 10:19-20 137
- Acts 13:2-4 138
- Acts 16:6, 7 138

PRINCIPLES: 138
- Rom. 8:1-5 138
- Rom. 8:13, 14 138
- I John 4:1-4 138
- I Tim. 4:1 138
- II Thess. 2:1, 2 138
- Acts 16:16-18 138
- Gal. 5:8 138
- Gal. 5:16-18 138

HIS PART IN OUR FAITH AND PRAYER 138

TABLE OF CONTENTS

    Heb. 11:1-3 139
    Heb. 11:6 139
    Heb. 11:32-38 139
    I Cor. 2:11-14 139
    Rom. 8:6-8 139
    Rom. 8:22-26 139
    Rom. 10:17 139
  SCRIPTURES: 139
    Eph. 6:17 139
    Rom. 8:26, 27 139
    Zech. 12:10 139
    Eph. 2:18 140
    Eph. 6:18 140
    Rom. 8:15 140
  SINS AGAINST THE HOLY SPIRIT 140
    Gen. 6:3 140
    Isa. 63:9, 10 140
    Mark 3:29, 30 140
    Acts 5:1-10 140
    Acts 7:51 140
    Eph. 4:30-32 140
    I Thess. 5:19 140
    Heb. 10:26-31 140

CHAPTER 6: MAN AND SIN **141**
OUR CREATION **141**
    I Cor. 2:14 141
    Heb. 11:3 141
    Rev. 4:11 141
    Heb. 2:6-8 141
    Gen. 1:1, 2 141

Gen. 1:26-28	141
Gen. 1:29-30	142
Gen. 2:7-9	142
Gen. 2:15-17	142
Gen. 2:18-20	142
Gen. 2:21-14	142
Eccl. 7:29	142
Eccl. 12:7	142
Matt. 10:28	142
Matt. 25:46	142
I Thess. 5:23	142
Our Fall	143
Rom. 5:12-21	143
Gen. 3:1	143
Gen. 3:2, 3	143
Gen. 3:4, 5	144
Gen. 3:6-11	144
Sin Nature	145
Psm. 51:4	145
Luke 15:18	145
Gal. 5:16-21	145
Rom. 7:14	145
DEFINITION OF SIN (14 DIFFERENT BIBLICAL ONES)	145
James 4:17 (1)	145
Jer. 14:7 (2)	145
Prov. 14:21 (3)	145
Prov. 21:4 (4)	146
Prov. 24:9 (5)	146
Num. 21:7 (6)	146
I Sam 15:23 (7 & 8)	146

TABLE OF CONTENTS

    Jer. 3:25 (9) 146
    John 16:8, 9 (10) 146
    Rom. 14:23 (11) 146
    I John 3:4 (12) 146
    Jas. 2:9 (13) 146
    I John 5:17 (14) 146
    PROGRESSION OF SIN 147
    Rom. 1:18 147
    Rom. 1:19-23 147
    Rom. 1:24-25 147
    Rom. 1:26-27 147
    Rom. 1:28-32 147
    RESULT OF SIN 147
    Rom. 8:22 147
    GOD – CREATOR 147
    MAN WAS CREATED A LITTLE LOWER THAN THE ANGELS 148
    Heb. 2:6, 7 148
    Rom. 8:22 148

CHAPTER 7: WHAT IS SALVATION? 149
    ABSOLUTE NEED TO BE SAVED 149
    Heb. 11:5, 6 149
    Acts 4:12 149
    John 3:7 149
    Gal. 6:15 149
    Eph. 2:1 149
    I Cor. 2:14 150
    Jer. 13:23 150
    Jer. 17:9, 10 150
    Luke 13:3, 5 150
    Luke 24:47, 48 150

Matt. 3:1, 2	150
Mark 6:12	150
Acts 26:20	150
John 3:16-18	151
John 3:36	151
THINGS WE ARE SAVED FROM	151
Matt. 16:24	151
Matt. 18:11	151
Mark 8:35	151
Luke 4:18	151
Luke 7:48-50	152
John 3:15-18	152
Acts 2:40	152
Rom. 5:8, 9	152
II Thess. 2:9-12	152
Heb. 2:15	152
Heb. 4:9-11	152
SALVATION IS ETERNAL	152
John 3:15, 16, 36	153
John 4:14	153
John 5:24	153
John 6:27	153
John 6:39, 40, 47, 54	153
John 6:68, 69	153
John 10:27, 28	153
John 11:25, 26	154
John 17:1-3	154
John 20:31	154
BY GRACE ALONE, THROUGH FAITH ALONE	154
Heb. 11:6	154

TABLE OF CONTENTS

Titus 2:11 154
Eph. 2:4-10 154
John 1:12, 13 154
Rom. 1:16 154
Rom. 10:9-17 154
Gal. 3:22-29 155
Heb. 4:9-11 155
I John 5:4 155
I John 5:11-13 155
James 2:14-26 155
Rom. 12:3 155
Heb. 12:2 155
A FULL (COMPLETE) SALVATION 155
I Thess. 5:23 155
I Thess. 5:5 156
I Thess. 4:7 156
II Cor. 5:17 156
II Cor. 7:10, 11 156
II Cor. 5:20 156
Rev. 1:5, 6 156
Acts 26:18 157
Matt. 16:24 157
John 14:16, 17 157
Rom. 8:9 157
Rom. 8:14 157
Rom. 8:16 157
Rom. 8:35-39 157
Titus 2:11-14 157
Rom. 6:23 158
Eph. 2:1 158

John 3:16	158
I Pet. 1:3-5	158
I John 1:3	158
I John 1:7, 9	158
I John 2:3	158
I John 3:14	159
I John 5:4	159
Heb. 10:38, 39	159
SALVATION IS THROUGH JESUS AND HIS WORK ALONE	159
John 14:6	159
Acts 4:12	159
John 1:12	159
John 1:29	159
John 3:14-21	159
Acts 16:31	160
Rom. 5:6-11	160
Rom. 6:23	160
Rom. 10:9, 10	160
I Cor. 15:3, 4	160
Gal. 3:26-29	160
Gal. 4:4, 5	160
Eph. 1:7	160
Eph. 2:10, 13	161
I John 5:11, 12	161
Rev. 5:8-10	161
John 5:39	161
Luke 24:25-27, 44	161
NATURE OF SAVING FAITH	161
Heb. 11:6	161
John 2:23-25	161

TABLE OF CONTENTS

    John 12:42-43 161
    Acts 8:13-23 162
    James 2:19, 20 162
    John 1:12, 13 162
    Eph. 2:8-10 162
    Gal. 1:23 162
    Gal. 2:16 162
    Gal. 2:20 162
    Gal. 3:22, 24, 25 162
    Heb. 11:1-3 163
    Heb. 11:4-39 163
    James 2:14, 17, 20, 26 163

CHAPTER 8: WHAT IS THE CHURCH? 165
    THE CHURCH 165
    UNIVERSAL AND LOCAL 165
    Eph. 1:22, 23 165
    I Thess. 1:1 165
    Gal. 1:2 165
    Acts 15:13-18 166
    Acts 16:5 166
    Matt. 16:13-18 166
    Matt. 18:15-17 166
    Eph. 5:22-33 166
    Eph. 3:3-11 167
    I Cor. 12:12, 13 167
    I Cor. 12:27-31 167
    Col. 1:13-18 167
    PURPOSE AND FUNCTION 167
    Eph. 2:19-22 167
    Eph. 3:7-10 167

Eph. 3:20, 21	168
Eph. 4:7-16	168
I Cor. 12:28	169
Acts 20:28	169
Acts 16:5	169
Acts 2:41	169
Acts 2:47	169
Eph. 5:21-23	169
II Cor. 11:2	170
Acts 12:5	170
Eph. 6:18, 19	170
Phil. 1:9, 10	170
Phil. 1:19	170
I Cor. 6:1-5	171
Phil. 4:10-19	171
Acts 13:1-5	171
Matt. 9:37, 38	171
I Tim. 3:5	171
I Tim. 3:14, 15	172
Heb. 2:11, 12	172
James 2:1-9	172
CHURCH DISCIPLINE	172
Matt. 18:15-17	172
Acts 5:1-10	173
Rom. 16:17, 18	173
I Cor. 5:1-13	173
I Cor. 11:16	173
I Thess. 5:14	173
II Thess. 3:6-15	174
I Tim. 1:19, 20	174

TABLE OF CONTENTS

    I Tim. 5:19, 20 174
    Titus 3:10, 11 174
    OFFICERS OF THE CHURCH 175
    Titus 1:5-11 (cf. I Tim. 3:1-7) 175
    II Tim. 3:8-13 176
    THE CHURCH AND THEIR PASTOR 176
    I Thess. 5:12-14 176
    Eph. 4:11-16 176
    Heb. 13:17, 7 177
    Psm. 105:15 177
    I Sam. 24:6, 10; 26:9, 11, 23 177
    II Sam. 1:14-16 177
    I Cor. 9:7-14 177
    I Tim. 5:17-20 177
    II Tim. 4:2-5 177

CHAPTER 9: THE CHRISTIAN LIFE 179
    A LIFE OF RIGHTEOUSNESS 179
    Isa. 64:6 179
    Rom. 3:9-12 179
    Titus 3:5, 6 179
    Titus 2:11-15 179
    Rev. 19:7-9 179
    Matt. 22:1-14 180
    I Cor. 1:26-31 180
    Rom. 3:20-26 180
    James 2:21-26 180
    I Pet. 4:17, 18 180
    I John 2:29 181
    I John 3:7 181
    Rom. 10:1-10 181

Rom. 6:9-13	181
Rom. 6:18, 19	181
Phil. 3:3-9	181
SAVED AND SEPARATE FROM THE WORLD	182
THIS WORLD IS CONTROLLED BY SATAN AND DEMONS	182
John 12:30-32	182
John 12:47, 48	182
John 14:30	182
John 16:7-11	182
II Cor. 4:3, 4	182
Eph. 6:12	182
I John 4:4	183
Rev. 12:9	183
Eph. 2:1, 2	183
I John 2:2, 15-17	183
II Tim. 4:10	183
James 4:4	183
II Pet. 2:19-22	183
I John 5:18, 19	184
Gal. 1:3, 4	184
Matt. 5:14	184
Luke 16:8	184
John 15:18, 19	184
John 16:33	184
John 17:9-16 – HIGH PRIESTLY PRAYER	184
Rom. 12: 1, 2	185
I Cor. 4:9, 13	185
Titus 2:12	185
Heb. 11:7	185
Heb. 11:38	185

TABLE OF CONTENTS

I John 3:1 185
I John 3:13 185
I John 4:5, 6 185
Gal. 6:14 186
James 1:27 186
II Pet. 1:4 186
I John 5:4, 5 186
Eph. 2:8-10 186
Matt. 16:27 186
Rev. 20:12, 13 187
Rev. 22:12 187
Matt. 5:16 187
John 14:12 187
John 17:4 187
II Tim. 4:7 187
I Cor. 3:13-15 187
I Cor. 15:58 188
II Cor. 6:1 188
II Cor. 9:8 188
Phil. 2:12, 13 188
I Tim. 5:25 188
II Tim. 2:15 188
II Tim. 2:21 188
II Tim. 3:16, 17 189
Titus 2:14 189
Titus 3:8, 14 189
James 2:14-26 189
Rev. 14:13 189
Rev. 2:2, 5, 9, 13, 19, 23, 26; 3:1, 8, 15 189
John 6:28, 29 190

Acts 9:36-39	190
Acts 26:20	190
I Cor. 9:1	190
I Thess. 1:3	190
I Tim. 3:1	190
I Tim. 5:10	190
I Tim. 6:17-19	190
II Tim. 4:5	190
Titus 2:7, 8	190
Heb. 13:21	191
John 18:38	191
John 14:6	191
John 16:13	191
I John 4:5, 6	191
I John 5:6	191
I John 2:27	191
John 17:17	191
II Tim. 2:15	191
James 1:18	191
John 1:14	192
John 1:17	192
John 3:15-21	192
John 8:32	192
John 8:40-46	192
Rom. 3:6-8	192
II Cor. 4:1, 2	192
II Cor. 11:10	192
Gal. 4:16	192
Eph. 4:15	193
Eph. 4:25	193

TABLE OF CONTENTS

Eph. 5:9 193
Eph. 6:14 193
II Thess. 2:10-12 193
I Tim. 2:4 193
I Tim. 4:2-3 193
I Tim. 6:5 194
II Tim. 3:7 194
II Tim. 4:4 194
James 3:14-16 194
James 5:12 195
I John 1:6, 8 195
I John 2:4 195
I John 2:21 195
Eph. 5:22 195
Eph. 5:23, 24 196
Eph. 5:25 196
Eph. 5:31 196
I Pet. 3:1 196
I Pet. 3:2 196
I Pet. 1:3, 4 196
I Pet. 1:5, 6 196
I Pet. 1:7 197
I Tim. 3:2-7 197
I Tim. 3:8-12 197
I Tim. 5:8 197
I Tim. 5:14, 15 197
Titus 2:1-8 197
Gen. 3:16-19 197
Prov. 31:10-31 198
I Cor. 7:1, 2 198

I Cor. 7:10, 11	198
I Cor. 7:12-16	198
I Cor. 7:27-34	198
I Cor. 7:38-40	198
II Tim. 1:5	199
II Tim. 3:15	199
Luke 2:41-47, 52	199
Deut. 6:4-12	199
Psm. 78:1-8	199
Prov. 22:6	199
Eph. 6:1-4	200
Matt. 15:22-28	200
Prov. 22:6	200
Prov. 13:24	200
Prov. 19:18	200
Prov. 22:15	200
Prov. 23:13, 14	200
Prov. 29:15-17	201
SETTLING OF PERSONAL DIFFERENCES	201
Between Christians	201
I John 4:19-5:2	201
I Cor. 13:4-7	201
Rom. 12:9, 10, 14	201
Rom. 12:17-21	201
Matt. 5:22-24	202
Matt. 18:15-18	202
I Cor. 6:1-8	202
With the Lost	202
Matt. 5:38-48	202
A Life of Prayer	202

TABLE OF CONTENTS

Phil. 4:6 203
I Thess. 5:17 203
Luke 18:1 203
I John 1:3-7 203
Matt. 7:7 203
Rom. 8:34, 26 203
Eph. 6:18 203
Rom. 1:9 204
I Cor. 1:4 204
Acts 12:5 204
I Sam. 12:23 204
Acts 6:2-4 204
Col. 4:2:-4 204
II Thess. 3:1-2 204
Gal. 5:19-21 204
Gal. 5:22-23 205
Gal. 2:20 205
John 15:1-17 205
I Cor. 13:1-13 205
II John 1:6 206
I John 2:9, 10 206
I John 2:15-17 206
I John 3:1 206
I John 3:11-18 206
I John 4:7-5:3 206

CHAPTER 10: FUTURE THINGS **207**
    Future of the Lost 207
    John 3:15-20 207
    John 3:36 207
    Rom. 3:23 207

Rom. 5:8-10	207
Rom. 6:23	207
Luke 16:22, 23	207
Luke 16:24	207
Luke 16:25	207
Luke 16:26	207
Luke 16:27-31	207
Isa. 33:14	208
II Thess. 1:9	208
Rev. 14:10, 11	208
Rev. 20:1	208
Rev. 20:6	208
Rev. 20:11-15	208
Rev. 22:10, 11	208
Rev. 22:15	208
John 14:1-6	209
I Thess. 4:13-18	209
I Thess. 5:9	209
Rev. 4:1-11	209
Rev. 5:8-13	209
Heb. 9:27	209
Rom. 14:10-12	210
II Cor. 5:10-12	210
I Cor. 3:9-15	210
Rev. 19:1-6	210
Rev. 19:7-9	210
Rev. 19:11-21	210
Rev. 20:1-9	211
Rev. 20-10-15	211
Rev. 21:1, 2	211

TABLE OF CONTENTS

Rev. 21:22-27 211
I Thess. 4:13-18 211
I Thess. 5:9 211
II Thess. 2:7-12 211
Rev. 6:7-17 212
Rev. 7:14 212
Rev. 19:11-20 212
Rev. 20:1-3 212
Rev. 20:4-6 212
Rev. 20:7-10 212
Rev. 20:11-15 212
Rev. 21:1 212
Rev. 1:19 213
Rev. 1:1 213
Rev. 19:10 213
Heb. 1:1, 2 213
Matt. 24:1-3 213
II Pet. 1:20, 21 213
I Tim. 4:1-6 214
II Tim. 3:1-14 214
I John 2:18 214
II Peter 3:3-14 214
Rev. 22:7 214
Rev. 22:12 214
Rev. 22:20 214
TERMS OFTEN USED 215
REASONS FOR A PRE-MILLENNIAL, PRE-TRIBULATIONAL RAPTURE 215
I Thess. 4:13-18 215
Zech. 14:3-9 215
Rev. 19:11-16 216

Matt. 14:27-31	216
DANIEL'S VISION OF 70-WEEKS	216
Dan. 9:24-27	216
PRINCIPLE OF TEMPORARY SUSPENSION OF RELATIONSHIP	216
I Kings 6:1	216
Acts 13:18-21	216
BEGINNING OF THE 70-WEEKS	217
Dan. 9:25, 26	217
Neh. 2:1-6	217
Dan. 9:24-27	217
-ORIGIN	217
Gen. 12:1-3	217
Matt. 16:18	217
Rom. 7:1-6	217
Rom. 11:13-25	218
CONTRAST ISRAEL (WIFE OF GOD) AND CHURCH (BRIDE OF CHRIST)	218
Isa. 54:5-8	218
Jer. 3:1-18	218
Ezek. 16:32, 38	218
Hosea 2	218
Hosea 3:1-5	218
Eph. 5:22-32	218
Rev. 19:7-9	219
-TYPES IN GENESIS	219
TEACHING IN ACTS	219
Acts 1:6-8	219
Acts 2: 5, 22	219
Acts 2:46	219
Acts 8:5, 14	219
Acts 10:28	219

TABLE OF CONTENTS

Acts 10:45 220
Acts 11:1, 18 220
Acts 13:44-46 220
Acts 15:1, 7-11 220
Acts 18:6 220
Acts 28:25-29 220
-SALVATION AND CIRCUMCISION 220
John 4:22 220
Gal. 3:23-29 220
Col. 2:9-13 221
THREE SEPARATE JUDGMENTS 221
-JUDGMENT SEAT OF CHRIST 221
Rom. 14:10-12 – must give an account 221
II Cor. 5:9-11 – works judged, both good and bad 221
I Cor. 3:12-17 – only useful works survive 221
- JUDGMENT OF THE NATIONS 221
Matt. 25:32-46 221
-GREAT WHITE THRONE OF JUDGMENT 221
Rev. 20:11-15 221
John 5:28, 29 221
II Tim. 4:1 221
Rev. 20:4-6 221
THE CHURCH IN REVELATION 222
Rev. 1:11, 12, 20 – Church is on earth 222
Rev. 2:1, 7, 8, 11, 12, 17, 18, 23, 29 – Church is on earth 222
Rev. 3:1, 6, 7, 13, 14, 22 – Church is on earth 222
Rev. 22:16 – Next and last mention of Church 222
Rev. 6:10, 11 222
Rev. 6:17 222
I Thess. 5:9 222

Rev. 9:20-21	222
OFFER REPENTANCE AGAIN	222
Rev. 14:7; 16:9-11	222
Rev. 12:17	222
Rev.17:1	222
Rev. 18:1, 2, 5-8, 20, 24	222
Rev. 19:21-20:3	222
Rev. 11:2, 3	222
CHAPTER 11: SPIRITUAL GIFTS	**223**
I Cor. 12:1	223
I Cor. 12:2, 3	223
ONLY THOSE WHO SPEAK CORRECTLY OF JESUS ARE DOING SO BY THE HOLY GHOST	223
I Cor. 12:4-6	223
I Cor. 12:7	223
I Cor. 12:11, 18	224
I Cor. 12:8-10	224
I Cor. 12:28	224
I Cor. 13:1-3	224
I Cor. 12:29-30	224
I Pet. 4:10, 11	225
I Cor. 12:31	225
I Cor. 13:4-7	225
Eph. 4:7-16	225
Ex. 35:30-35	226
WRONG ATTITUDES ABOUT SPIRITUAL GIFTS	226
I Cor. 1:7	226
II Tim. 4:5	226
GIFTS ARE FOR PERSONAL USE AND ENJOYMENT	226
I Cor. 14:12	226

TABLE OF CONTENTS

I Cor. 14:37, 38 227
GIFTS AND THE BODY OF CHRIST 227
Rom. 12:4-6 227
I Cor. 12:11-18 227
I Cor. 12:19-24 227
I Cor. 12:25-28 227
I Cor. 12:7-11 227
SPECIFIC GIFTS GIVEN 227
WORD OF WISDOM 227
I Cor. 12:8 227
Gen. 41:46, 37-39 228
Ex. 36:1, 2 228
Deut. 34:9 228
I Kings 3:5-12, 28 228
Prov. 2:6, 7 228
II Pet. 3:15, 16 228
James 3:13-18, 1:5 228
WORD OF KNOWLEDGE 228
I Cor. 12:8 228
I Cor. 13:2 228
13:8-10 228
2:9-14 228
8:1 228
II Cor. 12:7 228
Matt. 16:13-17 228
Dan. 1:17, 20 228
2:19-23 228
Luke 8:10 228
II Tim. 2:7 228
FAITH 228

I Cor. 12:9	228
Eph. 2:8-10	228
Rom. 1:17	229
I Cor. 13:2	229
Heb. 11:8-19	229
Rom. 4:18-21	229
Acts 6:5, 8	229
7:54-60	229
Mark 4:35-41	229
Heb. 11:1	229
11:33	229
11:1-40	229
GIFTS OF HEALING (S)	229
I Cor. 12:9	229
12:28	229
12:30	229
Matt. 8:8, 13	229
Mark 5:28, 29	229
Mark 16:18	229
Luke 9:1-6	229
Acts 3:1-8	229
5:15, 16	229
9:41, 42	229
28:8, 9	230
James 5:14-20	230
WORKING OF MIRACLES	230
I Cor. 12:10	230
12:28	230
12:29	230
Luke 4:33-36	230

TABLE OF CONTENTS

9:1 230
Mark 16:15-18 230
Acts 6:8 230
8:5-8 230
19:11, 12 230
PROPHECY (PROPHETS) 230
I Cor. 12:10 230
Eph. 4:7-11 230
I Cor. 12:28, 29 230
Psm. 105:15 230
Eph. 2:19-22 231
Eph. 3:5 231
FUNCTION 231
Deut. 18:18, 19 231
II Kings 17:13 231
Acts 13:1 231
Acts 15:32-33 231
I Cor. 14:3 231
Num. 11:25-29 231
II Pet. 1:20, 21 231
I Cor. 14:24, 25 231
ADDITIONAL NOTES 232
Amos 3:7 232
Jer. 27:18 232
Jer. 25:4, 5 232
I Sam. 3:19, 20 232
DISCERNING OF SPIRITS 232
I Cor. 12:10 232
I John 4:1-6 232
Acts 16:16-18 232

Matt. 16:22, 23	232
I Cor. 14:29	233
I Cor. 6:1-8	233
APOSTLES	234
I Cor. 12:28, 29	234
Eph. 4:7-11	234
— APOSTLE COMES FROM A GREEK WORD.	234
Heb. 3:1	234
Luke 22:14	234
Acts 14:4, 14	234
Rom. 16:7 — Andronicus and Junia	234
I Cor. 4:6, 9 — Apollos and Sosthenes (1:1)	235
Eph. 2:19, 20	235
Eph. 3:1-7	235
FUNCTION	235
Acts 14:4	235
Acts 14:21, 22	235
Acts 14:23-28	235
CALLING	235
Gal. 1:1	235
Acts 13:1-4	235
Rom. 15:20	235
EVANGELISTS	236
Eph. 4:7-11	236
I Cor. 12:28, 29	236
Acts 21:8	236
II Tim. 4:5	236
PASTORS	236
Eph. 4:7-11	236
I Cor. 12:28, 29	236

TABLE OF CONTENTS

Acts 14:23	236
Acts 20:28-32	237
TEACHERS	237
I Cor. 12:28, 29	237
Eph. 4:7-11	237
Eph. 4:12-16	237
I Tim. 3:2	237
Titus 1:9-11	237
Acts 13:1-4	237
II Tim. 2:2	237
II Tim. 2:24-26	237
I Tim. 2:12	238
Titus 2:3-5	238
GIFT OF HELPS	238
I Cor. 12:1, 7, 11, 18	238
12:28	238
Ex. 18:22	238
Num. 11:14-17	238
Acts 20:35	238
SHOWING MERCY	238
Rom. 12:8	238
Matt. 9:27	238
15:22	238
17:15	238
20:30-34	238
Luke 10:30-37	238
17:13	239
Acts 9:39, 40	239
GIFTS OF "GIVING"	239
I Chron. 29:1-19	239

Rom. 12:3-8	239
John 12:2-8	239
II Cor. 8:1-9	239
:2	239
:3	239
:4	239
:5	239
:6	239
:7-8	239
:9	239
9:6-8	239
Phil. 4:15-19	239
EXHORTATION	239
Rom. 12:8	239
Acts 11:19-23	240
Acts 14:21, 22	240
Acts 15:31, 32	240
I Tim. 4:13	240
I Tim. 6:2	240
SUBJECTS ARE VARIED	240
Titus 1:9	240
II Thess. 3:12	240
I Tim. 2:1	240
I Pet. 5:1, 2	240
MANNER OF EXHORTING	240
I Thess. 2:11	240
I Thess. 5:14	240
II Tim. 4:2	240
Titus 2:15	240
Rom. 12:8	241

TABLE OF CONTENTS

I Tim. 3:4, 5, 12 241
I Thess. 5:12 241
Heb. 13:7, 17, 24 241
I Cor. 12:28 241
Titus 1:5 241
II Tim. 2:2 241
I Tim. 1:3 241
Rom. 12:7 242
Col. 1:7, 23, 25 242
II Tim. 1:16-18 242
Heb. 6:10 242
Acts 6:1-4 242
Matt. 20:26-28 242
I Pet. 4:10, 11 242
Philemon 13 242
II Cor. 11:15 242
I Cor. 16:15 242
HOSPITALITY 242
Rom. 12:13, 9 243
I Pet. 4:9-11 243
I Tim. 3:2 243
Titus 1:8 243
Heb. 13:2 243
Gen. 18:1-8 243

ABOUT THE AUTHOR 245

CHAPTER 1
THE SCRIPTURES

What a person believes about the Bible will determine what they will believe about the teachings of the Bible. A weakness in the doctrine of the Scriptures usually shows up in other areas later. The shallowness and heresies of our day are the result of wrong thinking about inspiration, preservation, interpretation, application, and the sufficiency of the Scriptures. Every cult and ism can be exposed at this point.

II Tim. 3:15-17

    Five purposes of Scriptures
    Salvation
    Doctrine
    Reproof
    Correction
    Instruction in Righteousness
    Sufficiency – What the Scriptures can do in and of themselves:
    "Able"
    "Perfect" well-rounded, properly balanced, fully prepared
    "All good works"
    Such adequacy does not require extra Biblical helps

    Origin – "of God"
    Inspiration
    Not to be confused with two other processes:
    Revelation – God revealing truths and/or His Son to us (**I Cor. 2:9,10; Matt. 11:25-27; 18:17**)
    Illumination – getting light, insight, and understanding on a given subject
    Opposite of expire (breathe out or lose breath of life)
    Breathe in the breath of life
    <u>Process</u> God used for giving Scriptures
    Not inspired men
    Inspired Scriptures

Similar to mouth-to-mouth resuscitation of drowning victims ... one breathes for the other, thus dominating the breathing
This process was used exclusively for Scripture

II Pet. 1:16-21

Scriptures are contrasted with devised fables
Scriptures are superior to personal experience, even that of the Mount of Transfiguration
Scriptures did not come by man's will
The Holy Ghost was the source and the force of inspiration
"moved" the man
God only used holy men

I Pet. 1:9-12

Men wrote and then tried to get understanding
Words, not thoughts, were given by God
Words would have to be God's words, not men's words (**Matt. 4:4**)
If, as some teach, God gave thoughts and men then put in their own words, obviously they would have understood what they wrote:
The Scriptures would be of no higher value than the intelligence of the writers
We would be robbed of the preciseness and clarity of the Scriptures, for they could then have been written in a multitude of ways as long as the thought might be found therein

I Thess. 2:13

The Bible is <u>God's</u> Word, not man's word
The Bible is to be received as God's Word
Salvation is tied to our attitude towards the Scriptures (**Prov. 13:13**).

Matt. 22:29

Ignorance of the Scriptures leads to error (**Hosea 4:1-14**)
Jesus expected people to have a working knowledge of the Old Testament

II Pet. 3:15, 16 – Wrong attitude or use of Scriptures brings destruction

Rev. 22:18, 19

Danger of adding to the Scriptures
Danger of taking away from the Scriptures

CHAPTER 1: THE SCRIPTURES

God is obviously finished writing Scriptures

Matt. 15:1-6
Two foundations of belief
Tradition
Scripture
Jesus sided with Scripture against tradition
Religious leaders had used tradition to avoid the commands of Scripture

Luke 16:29-31
Sufficiency of Scriptures to bring sinners to repentance
Scriptures have more authority than one returning from the dead

Luke 24:25-27
Jesus expected a belief in <u>all</u> of the Scriptures (as written)
<u>All</u> the Scriptures speak of Jesus
We should so study that we could start at any place and point someone to Jesus
There is far more to Jesus than most people suspect

Luke 24:44-49
We need God's help to have our understanding opened
Our ministry must be preceded by getting an understanding from the Scripture
The extent of our ministry is related to our understanding of the Scripture

John 5:39, 45-47
Scriptures alone can't save
The Scriptures alone tell of Jesus who can save.
Study to see Jesus
Doubt one part and you cannot believe in Jesus
Especially this applies to the first five books of the Bible including Creation, Fall, Flood, Law, Miracles, etc.

I Cor. 2:9-14
Scriptures are taught by God Himself (**I John 2:20, 27**)
Believers only can get a proper under-standing

Heb. 1:1-3
The Bible is progressive in revelation
Consider the progress in the prophecies of Jesus

Consider the Bible:
Unique in trustworthiness: no conflict with science, geography, racial history, chronological history, biographical history, events of history – archeology never contradicts it

Unique in subject matter: sin, sinners, sovereign God, hell, salvation, prophecy, miraculous, Saviour, judgment, view of evil, view of the world

Unity of purpose: 66 books, 40+ authors (prince, King, priest, farmer, shepherd, doctor, slave, tax-collector prisoner, fisherman, tentmaker), 3 languages, 3 continents, 16 centuries, various cultures (Egyptian, Jewish, Syrian, Medeo-Persian, Babylonian, Roman)

Fulfillment of prophecy – in precise accuracy, great detail, given long before flow of events in that direction; includes the miraculous happening, etc.

Lives changed by its teachings

Preservation principle: against great foes, Israel as a people, the Church as a witness, and the Scriptures themselves!

Amos 8:11, 12
Prophetic passage telling of future problem
Coming famine of the "**the words of the Lord**"
No evidence of a shortage of religion
Desire for the Word is present but the supply Is gone

Jer. 23:30
God's Words are stolen from people
Perhaps something much weaker is left in its place
The stealing is done by religious leaders who are near, or neighbors to those stolen from
God is "against" all that would remove the actual words of God from us

II Cor. 2:17
The corruption of God's Word was well underway in Paul's day
The majority seemed to be for corruption
The position for purity of God's Word seems to have been held by the minority even then

I Pet. 1:23, 25
The Scriptures are necessary for one to be "**born again.**"

CHAPTER 1: THE SCRIPTURES

Some of the traits of the "**Word of God**" (by which people are saved) are:
not corruptible but incorruptible
liveth forever
abideth forever
endureth forever
There must be two kinds; pure and corrupt
God blesses that which is pure

Matt. 7:15-20

Interpretation is obviously regarding ministers.
Fruits reveal either a good or corrupt source.
While this involves the nature of the minister, it can also well apply to the nature of the ministry.
Use of good Bibles will produce different results than the use of corrupt Bibles.

Psm. 119:89

God's Word is a settled matter – unchangeable
David said it was settled (more than 3000 years ago)
The "settling" is a matter of <u>forever</u> – past, present, future
never been unsettled
never will be unsettled
Location of the settling is in heaven

Psm. 119:160

God's Word has always been true
God's Word has existed from the beginning
God's judgments will <u>all</u> survive and stand the test of time – endure forever

Psm. 138:2

God has "*magnified*" His Word
God cares more about His Word than His Name
Consider Commandment #3 and (**Rev. 22:18, 19**)

Matt. 5:18

O.T. Law is safe in accuracy
Jot and tittle are Hebrew letter markings
God won't allow the change of a letter, much less the change of a word or phrase

Mark 13:31 (also Luke 21:33)
>Words of Jesus are safe in accuracy
>Jesus' Words can never be destroyed

Luke 16:17
>Difficulty in changing one letter of the Law
>Law will continue, – not fail

John 10:35b
>"Scripture cannot be broken"
>The Bible is a unit not to be broken into pieces
>Scripture must be fulfilled (**Acts 13:29**)

John 17:17
>Bible is to be trusted
>Not only full of truth; but is truth in and of itself
>One of the answers to Pilate's question, "***What is truth?***" (**John 18:38a**)

Psm. 119:140
>Purity claimed for Scriptures
>Purity of unquestionable character, - "***very pure***"

Psm. 12:6, 7
>Purity is complete, – like the finest silver
>God guarantees the preservation of the very word<u>s</u>, forever

Consider the versions:

All English Bibles are translations of either pure or corrupt Scriptures – Hebrew, Chaldean, and Greek
Biggest area of difference today is in the N.T., the O.T. also has much variance
Contrast Greek Manuscripts
quantity
age
condition
location
material
style of Greek
origin
Source of manuscripts, who accepts which, who used which etc.

CHAPTER 1: THE SCRIPTURES

Fruit of various manuscripts – Hidden Seed, Reformation, Fundamentalism, Evangelism, Missions, Colleges, Seminaries, Power, Holiness, Separation, Liberalism, Faith Ministries, Neo-Evangelicalism, approach to interpretation of Scriptures
Changes and their influence on doctrine – Virgin Birth, Deity of Jesus, Miracles, Trinity, Blood Atonement, Lordship, Repentance, Fastings, Resurrection, Faith, Incarnation, and more.
Motives for new versions

Eph. 6:17
Word belongs to the Holy Spirit
Likened to a sword, - offensive part of our armour

Psm. 119:9
Word can cleanse our way
Cleansing comes from listening to and obeying the Word

Psm. 119:11
Word to be memorized
One purpose of memorization is to keep from sinning
Sinning is against <u>God</u>

Psm. 119:63
Individual response to the Word sets the bounds of fellowship
Obedience makes for companions
Disobedience costs closeness to those who continue to obey

Psm. 119:72
Scriptures to be highly valued by us
Scriptures to be chosen as better than great wealth
Must never choose money over the Scriptures speaking to us

Psm. 119:105
Word gives us light to live by
Idea is a foot lamp that lights the path one step at a time

Psm. 119:126
The Law is a necessity for Revival
Need and time for Revival is evidenced by others making "**void**" (or of no use), the Law of God

Psm. 119:126
    The Scriptures can produce peace.
    The Law is tied to peace – it settles issues for us
    Peace is great when we <u>love</u> God's law
    Sufficient love produces peace that ends in <u>nothing</u> offending us

RULES OF BIBLE INTERPRETATION

II Tim. 2:15
    Scriptures are to be divided, but not broken
    The division must be done rightly and not wrongly
    It takes much study and work
    Wrongly dividing produces shame
    Rightly dividing brings God's approval

Mark 7:9, 13
    We must never allow men's command-ments (decrees, laws, writings, commentaries, etc.) to become doctrine. They often can confuse our understanding of the Bible.
    Men's traditions (religious, cultural, social, and historical, etc.) are no help to understanding the Bible.
    Men's commandments and traditions often replace or make void the Word of God.

Jer. 23:36
    We are not to change the obvious meaning of God's Word<u>s</u>
    God meant what He said or He would have said it otherwise
    God has never been incapable of communicating clearly to humans

II Cor. 4:2
    God's Word is to be handled honestly
    We must never misuse or deceive to win an argument

Heb. 4:2
    Not all people benefit the same from the Scriptures – some get no profit
    The problem is not with the Scriptures or the speaker, but with the hearer
    God's Word is to be mixed with faith when heard and studied

CHAPTER 1: THE SCRIPTURES

II Pet. 3:16

God's Word is to be left as stated, and not wrested or twisted into some other meaning.

Unlearned and unstable individuals are particularly tempted to try to twist Scriptures which they don't understand.

Twisting or wresting Scriptures from its context and the rest of the Bible brings destruction

I Tim. 6:20

Avoid the opposition of counterfeit sciences (true science will always agree with the Bible)

Avoid the common, corrupt, and/or proud babblings (noise without substance, circular reasoning, and illogical statements) that attack the Bible

I Pet. 1:11

Writers took literally what God had them write

They didn't strain, charge, or maim what God said, but took their own lack of understanding as an evidence of their own ignorance. They then set out to study and try to grasp how things could happen as God had said.

Anything that can be taken literally should be taken as written.

People who spiritualize Scripture usually have no spiritual eyes and end up telling spiritual lies.

God said what He meant and meant what He said.

We believe God's Word whether we understand it or not. Don't try to bring Scripture down to your understanding.

Any Scripture has only one correct interpretation ... though it may have several possible applications.

Applications can never violate or annul Bible teaching through interpretations.

Never use applications, parables, allegories, types, etc. as the foundation for teaching. They only illustrate what God stated clearly.

I I Pet. 1:20

No one person can interpret for everybody

No one is free to interpret Scripture as he pleases

No Scripture can be interpreted separately from all of the rest of Scripture

James 1:22

God's Word – to be heard and lived

Hearing without living is self-deception

Luke 24:25

All Scripture is to be believed
All Scripture is to be taken as given
Often it takes an act of God to get us to believe what we should have trusted all along (**John 2:22**)
Right worship is tied to full belief of all the Scriptures (**Acts 24:14**)

Eph. 6:17

Bible belongs to God
It is God's Word, not men's thoughts
God said it as He wanted it
Who can say it better than God? Who is more accurate than God? Who is clearer than God? Who can say it more powerfully than God? Who better knows how to say enough without saying too much?
God's Word talks to us. We are to listen, obey, and live it.
Consider: Context: Who speaks, Who is spoken to, Rest of Scriptures on the subject
Fulfilled prophecies of Scripture were always fulfilled literally!
One Scripture doesn't contradict other Scriptures (John 10:35)
The Bible is its own best commentary
Error is usually not the opposite of truth, but rather one part of the truth taken to an extreme at the neglect of the rest of truth.

Rev. 1:20

God often defines the terms used as pictures
These explanations are to be taken literally

Mark 4:1-20

Jesus occasionally explained parables
These explanations are to be taken literally

Daniel 8:1-27

Dreams and visions were often explained
Take these explanations literally

Gal. 4:22-31

Allegories were sometimes explained
Take these explanations literally
Understand the following and the differences between:
Dreams

CHAPTER 1: THE SCRIPTURES

    Visions
    Parables
    Illustrations
    Allegories
    Types
    Anti-types
    Comparisons
    Word Pictures
    Understand how to recognize each of the above
    Understand the use of each of the above
    Watch out for the abuse of each of the above

John 5:46, 47
    Jesus expected us to take the Bible literally
    Unbelief in Scriptures brings unbelief in Jesus' words
    John 2:17, 22 – The disciples learned to take the Bible literally
    Acts 20:35 – The Apostle Paul took the Scriptures literally
    Acts 7:37 – Stephen took the Scriptures literally
    Acts 2:16-18, 25-31 – Peter took the Scriptures literally
    James 2:10, 11 – James took the Scriptures literally
    Rev. 3:7 – John took the Scriptures literally (**Isa. 22:22**)
    Daniel 9:1-4 – Daniel took the Scriptures literally (**Jer. 25:11, 12**)

How else would you normally approach a book, literature, accounts, or a letter?

WAYS TO LEARN FROM THE BIBLE

The Bible is like a gold mine. Its precious treasures require your effort and taking of planned steps if you are to make them your own. Otherwise they will lie there waiting for someone else to discover, and you will remain poor.

CONSIDER YOUR DESIRES AND ATTITUDES:

I Pet. 2:2
    The Word must be desired
    We must seek as a newborn babe desires milk
    We should yearn to grow

Rom. 15:4
> <u>All</u> Scripture is practical and for our benefit
> We must approach the Scriptures with patience

Psm. 119:10
> We should seek God through the Scriptures with our whole heart
> We should watch and pray that we do not wander from His commandments

Psm. 119:103
> We should learn the taste of the Scriptures – sweet!
> It requires chewing, absorbing, – not swallowing quickly

I Thess. 4:11
> Quietness to learn is needed
> We must study on how to get quiet
> Devotions are often called "*The Quiet Time with God*"

WE MUST TAKE TIME TO HEAR FROM GOD:

Psm. 119:147, 148
> Before sunrise
> Throughout the night
> Don't restrict learning time to a few moments a day
> Trust the Word in the morning and meditate on it at night
> confidence for actions
> reflection on God's Word as applied to the day's activities

WE SHOULD HAVE A PLAN:

Psm. 119:18, 27, 28
> Ask God for help in learning
> Pray for strength

Psm. 119:15
> Meditate on God's Word
> think it over
> compare with other Scriptures
> chew on it until it becomes part of you

CHAPTER 1: THE SCRIPTURES

Psm. 119:11
Memorize it
Have it not only in your head, but also in your heart to govern your life's decisions and emotions

Psm. 119:7
Bible is to be learned
Learning is usually best when accomplished three different ways:

Reading
reading through the Bible chapter by chapter, book by book, just as it is written
this will give you a general idea of its contents the first several times
after a while, you will get a feel for certain books and begin to grasp the relationship of various truths

Devotional
taking a certain passage and letting the truths seep into our souls
often this will come from some verse or verses God impressed on you as you go through your Bible readings
devotional guides are a help but should never replace the Holy Spirit's speaking directly to your soul from the pure Word

Studying
this requires great effort but helps us stay out of error and rightly divide the Word (**II Tim. 2:15**).
there is a variety of approaches and a blend is better than using only one style:
Read a book or chapter through 10-100 times
outline
find key thoughts, words, ideas, themes
find relationships etc.
Trace a word, principle, or doctrine through a book or the Bible
Study a person, place, or thing

LET GOD THE HOLY SPIRIT TEACH YOU:

John 14:26
The Holy Spirit is our teacher
He can teach us <u>all</u> things

I John 2:27
    The Holy Spirit is always right
    We must learn to abide in Him
    more on this subject under the study of the doctrine of the Holy Spirit

CHAPTER 2
WHO IS GOD?

GOD

I Cor. 2:9-16

    God nor His things are understood by the human mind (**11**)
    God nor His things are understood naturally (**14**)
    The Holy Ghost must teach us of God (**13**)
    It takes a knowledge of the spiritual to learn of a spiritual God (**13, 14**)
    God is greater than His creation
    infinite God
    finite man

Heb. 11:5, 6

    Two conditions must be met before we can come to God …
    belief in His existence
    belief in His nature as a "rewarder of them that <u>diligently</u> seek Him"
    God cannot be pleased unless we exercise faith in Him

Rom. 10:17

    We do not naturally have the necessary faith
    We cannot earn, buy, deserve, or produce the needed faith
    Faith must come to us
    Faith comes to us by a specific process
    God's Word is necessary for faith and therefore for a knowledge of God
    It is <u>not</u> hearing <u>of</u> the Word of God, but the hearing <u>by</u> the Word of God, – God speaks through His Word! We must listen for God to speak.

Rom. 1:18-32

    God has revealed Himself
    truth had but held wrong (**18**)
    inward manifestation by God Himself (**19**)
    creation demonstrates outwardly His power and Godhead for all to see (**20**)
    Man has rejected the true God and changed to a weak false god (**21-23**)

God releases us to go deeper into sin as we reject the truth (**24-25**) (**26-27**) (**28-32**)
Mankind and individuals are without excuse for not worshipping God (**20b**)

Psm. 14:1-3

Fool says <u>in heart</u> – no God
may not say it with mouth
may not be "there is no God", but "no God" in this part of my life, or "no God" will tell me what to do, etc.
Avoiding or denying God is foolish
Leaving God out of our thoughts is a mark of the wicked (**Psm. 10:4, 53:1**)

Gen. 1:1

When Time began (at the beginning) God already existed. He pre-dates Time.
Bible does not try to prove God's existence
Bible starts with God, and then with Time

John 17:3

Eternal life involves a personal knowing of God
No knowing, no salvation
God has many unique traits or attributes

ETERNAL

Gen. 21:33

Everlasting God
Will never come to an end

Ex. 3:13, 14

Constantly existing
Always in the present, – never past or future tense
He created us to live where He does – present tense

Deut. 33:27

Called the "eternal" God
Neither beginning nor ending

Psm. 90:2

Always been and shall be God

CHAPTER 2: WHO IS GOD?

From everlasting to everlasting – infinite distance to past and future
From everlasting to everlasting – simple definition of eternity

Psm. 102:24-27
God has no end
Heaven and earth are temporary in time and shall be treated like worn out clothes
God's being a refuge keeps us from thinking in an earth-bound fashion

Heb. 1:10-12
God started the beginning by creating the earth and the heavens
God maintains His sameness through all eternity

Isa. 44:6
First and last
Redeemer is eternal in being
Nothing before Him and nothing after Him
He encompasses all of time

Isa. 57:15
Eternity is God's dwelling place
Time without limit is filled by God
God is not bound by time but lives in all of it at once
> i.e., To God, the flood is happening, Israel is leaving Egypt, Goliath is being defeated, Paul is preaching, you are studying, and the Rapture is occurring, etc.

Surely our God is beyond our understanding time-wise, and worthy of our worship and awe!

GOD IS SPIRIT

John 4:23, 24
God, by nature, is a spirit
Our ties to the physical, sensual, and emotional will not touch God
We must operate in the spiritual realm if we are to contact God in worship
Only actions in the spiritual which are controlled by truth will succeed. Error will make even spiritual acts fail to produce right worship.

Luke 24:39
> A spirit is different from a body
> Bodies can be seen and touched
> God's presence is not seen nor felt by the physical senses
> Jesus, as eternal God and Spirit in being, took on a physical body for our sakes at a given point in time

John 1:18
> God, by nature a spirit, cannot be seen, and therefore has never been seen
> God, embodied in human form was not seen, but the human form was seen, touched, etc. (**I John 1:1, 2**).

John 14:7-10
> God is seen, not in His being (spirit), but as manifested in life, action, deeds, and works
> Jesus is the great demonstration of God to an unseeing world
> All to be seen of the Father is seen in Jesus the Son
> The spirit (invisible) is shown through the outworking in the flesh (visible). This is true in Jesus, and also applies to the Christian.

GOD HAS ALL KNOWLEDGE (OMNISCIENCE)

Rom. 11:32-36
> God's knowledge runs deep
> God's knowledge is unsearchable, beyond our learning

I John 3:20
> God knows "all things"
> "Knoweth" is continual, always has and always will know everything

Psm. 147:4, 5
> God has numbered all the stars
> He even has names for each star
> Understanding is without limits – infinite

Psm. 139:1-4
> God knows even such insignificant things like our sitting down and getting up

CHAPTER 2: WHO IS GOD?

    God keeps track even of our fleeting and distant thoughts
    God knows all our paths, habits, and ways of doing things
    God knows even the unspoken words that never leave our tongue

Prov. 15:3
    God sees everywhere
    God keeps track of both good and evil

Acts 15:18
    God not only knows everything about the Universe and us, – He also knows all of His own actions from creation forward
    God is never caught by surprise
    God's complete foreknowledge does <u>not</u> remove man's responsibility

GOD NEVER CHANGES (IMMUTABILITY)

Mal. 3:6
    God doesn't change
    Our future security rests on God's staying the same

James 1:17
    God doesn't vary or turn in nature, even a little
    God's gifts to us and our salvation rest on God's consistency

Num. 23:19
    God is vastly different from mankind
    God neither lies nor repents
    God always keeps His Word

Heb. 6:13-20
    Promises will be fulfilled though we may need to be patient (**vs. 15**)
    "Immutable" means no change
    This is a basis for consolation to the believer

Heb. 13:8
    Jesus is the same always
    This makes for a consistency of doctrine and practice (**vss. 7, 9**)

Jonah 3:9, 10
    God's turning and repenting here is evidence of the consistency of His nature
    He is consistently against the wicked

Their repentance with suitable fruits meant they were no longer rebels, and thus were removed from those whom God was against. Thus, God's change toward them was His staying the same towards sin and righteousness – consistency in nature. The real change was in the people who moved from those appointed to wrath over to those appointed to mercy.

Gen. 6:5-7

This is again evidence of the unchangeableness of God
Man created (**Gen. 1:26, 27, 31**) in the image of God had been pronounced good
Now man is debased in image and pronounced wicked
Man, by sin, has turned his back on the place of blessing and chosen the place of judgment. Man has changed places while God stays the same towards obedience and disobedience. For God not to change His
dealings with changed men would be inconsistent with His nature and justice.

EXAMPLE

The government is to honor the good and punish the evil. If a good man becomes evil, he should expect a change of treatment from the unchanging law. He has changed, – the gov't remains the same.

GOD HAS ALL POWER (OMNIPOTENCE)

Matt. 19:16-26

Man is limited – some things are impossible to him (**26**)
salvation is beyond man's power
God is not limited
all things are possible to Him
He can and does save

Jer. 32:27, 17

Some would ask if anything is too hard for the Lord (**Gen. 18:14**)
Nothing is beyond His power
Creation is an example of His power

Gen. 17:1

One name for God is "the Almighty God"
God's might should help us

In our daily walk
In perfecting those areas we lack in
In trusting His covenant promises

Job 42:1, 2
God has no limits
He not only can do anything, but even more – everything
We should learn this as it will humble us

Dan. 4:35
God is so powerful that no one can stop Him or hold Him back
His power allows Him to do all His will in heaven and earth
Even the heathen need to see this truth and may go on through difficult times to learn this lesson (see the context)

Rev. 19:6
Omnipotent means all-powerful
His power is the basis of His reigning in the future

EXAMPLES OF HIS POWER:

Creation of the Universe
Events of men
Events in Heaven
Control of Satan
Prophecy fulfilled

GOD IS ALL PRESENT (OMNIPRESENT)

Main residence in heaven, but spirit being everywhere

Psm. 139:7-11
God's existence reaches from heaven to hell
There is nowhere we can go to escape God's presence
Distance and time cannot remove us from God's presence
Anywhere He is well able to lead, protect, and hold us!

I Kings 8:27
God is too big to be contained in a building, on the earth, or even in the heavens
God is not like man in size or limitations, He has no physical limits, but fills all space that exists
The "bigness" of God is beyond our minds' ability to grasp

Jer. 23:23, 24
> No one can hide from God (Jonah tried and failed)
> There is nowhere on earth but what our God is God
> This should encourage us in witnessing, sending missionaries, and praying for the lost

Matt. 18:20
> God's presence is assured for Believers gathered in Christ's Name without limits on location or number meeting at one time.
> God is able to be in the midst many places at once
> While everywhere in a general sense, He is especially present in particular places

John 14:23
> God dwells with individuals (**17 and 20**)
> The special sense of abiding, indwelling is for those who meet God's conditions
> This is different from His general presence everywhere; in nature, blessing, intensity, purpose, protection, etc.

Acts 17:24-28
> God by nature is close at hand to the lost
> Our lives are surrounded by His existence as well as evidence of His being

John 20:17
> Father's main location is heaven
> Jesus has joined Him there

Results:
> Comforting truth of His presence
> Holy Spirit's indwelling
> Ease of detection of good and bad

GOD IS HOLY

I Pet. 1:16
> God claims to be holy (**Lev. 19:2**)
> God commands us to be holy because He is holy

Isa. 6:3-7
> God is thrice Holy – fully so and each member of the Trinity

God's holiness is perhaps His leading or most emphasized trait (attribute)
God's holiness is related to His glory and our cleansing

Rev. 4:8
God's holiness is emphasized in both Old Testament and New Testament
God's holiness is emphasized in heaven and should be on earth

Heb. 12:14
Holiness is expected in mankind
Without holiness we shall never see God

Lev. 11:43-45
God's holiness is the basis of His demands for holiness in our lives
Our <u>separation</u> from the World (Egypt), <u>from</u> the flesh (the unclean), and <u>to</u> serve God (sanctification), are all based on God's holiness.

I John 1:5
Holiness is likened to light
No unholiness or darkness in God
Basis of fellowship with man (**vss. 6, 7**)

Psm. 99:9
God's holiness should lead us to worship
Worship is tied to exalting God

John 17:11
Holy is part of the <u>Father's Name</u>
God's holiness is related to His keeping power
Perfect holiness makes for permanent keeping of the saints!

Acts 3:14
"Holy One" is one of the names of Jesus
Jesus' holiness is related to why He was rejected and crucified
Men today still choose murderers over holy people for friends

Eph. 4:13
We are to be changed into "the stature of the fullness of Christ"
Such practical holiness is a product of a local church operating properly

Rom. 1:4
> Holy Spirit is called the "Spirit of holiness"
> One of His Ministries is to produce holiness in believers

Hab. 1:12, 13
> God is eternal, almighty, and holy
> His holiness will not let Him look, stare, behold, gaze, or absorb that which is evil.
> We are also to be holy (**Job 31:1**)

GOD IS A TRINITY

tri-unity, three in one, one in three
This is not based on reason, but on revelation

I John 5:7
> Three in heaven
> "Three are one", yet obviously also three
> God is beyond our intelligence (**Rom. 11:33**)
> This truth is denied by several heresies

Unitarians	Mormons
Apostolics	Jehovah's Witnesses
Liberals	Tritheism
Polytheism	Swedenborgianism

I Cor. 13:12
> Some matters are not clear to our present understanding
> This doesn't change them, but does let us know there will be better understanding later
> Several illustrations of the Trinity are helpful, but inadequate:
> egg – shell, white, yolk
> triangle – three sides
> government – judicial, legislative, executive
> matter – gas, liquid, solid
> dimensions – height, length, breadth
> fire – heat, fuel, air
> man – spirit, soul, body
> offices of a man – father, husband, son
> authority – family, local church, government
> ministries – prophet, priest, king

CHAPTER 2: WHO IS GOD?

Matt. 28:19, 20
    Only Bible picture of the Trinity to the best of my knowledge
    One baptism, three persons, and three dips
    Thus three are one and one is three
    Each member of the Godhead is honored equally, jointly, yet separately for their part in redemption
    The two aspects of the Trinity and here combined in picture, i.e. unity and three being one

[Historically, single immersion was introduced in the 4th century by the Eunomius, an Arian sect, who denied the Trinity and wanted to destroy the picture. Unfortunately, this form has been copied by many well-meaning Christians of the West who are ignorant of its origin. "Theodoret, the author of an ecclesiastical history, and other works, and who lived in the early part of the fourth century, has the following testimony in regard to the change in the mode of immersion, and the form of words used in administering it: 'He (Eunomius) subverted the law of holy baptism, which had been handed down from the Lord and the apostles, and made a contrary law, asserting that it is not necessary to immerse the candidate for baptism thrice, nor to mention the names of the Trinity, but to immerse once only into the death of Christ.' --Chrystal's History of the Modes of Baptism, page 78." (James Quinter, *Triune Immersion*, Brethren Publishing House, Elgin, IL, 1907, pp. 82-83]

UNITY

Deut. 6:4, 5
    We only have one God, not three
    He is to be loved heart (spirit), soul, and might (body) (**Mark 12:29, 30**)

Isa. 44:6
    Only one God
    Both King <u>and</u> Redeemer are LORD
    Both King <u>and</u> Redeemer are one "I AM"
    First and Last (Rev. 1:17; 22:13)
    There is no other God
    (Isa. 44:8; 45:5, 6, 18, 21, 22; 46:9)

John 10:27-33

Jesus taught the unity of the Godhead
(vs. 30)
The Jews rejected a Godhead for a single personhood of God. They rejected Jesus' being God.

I Tim. 2:5

Jesus was God and a mediator between God and man
Yet God is only one - unified

Mark 10:17, 18

The rich young ruler needed to grasp, by revelation, that Jesus was God also, yet, there is only one God.

THREE IN ONE

Gen. 1:26, 27

God speaks among Himself
He uses words such as "us" and "our" to express His plurality (**vs. 26**)
Creation in His likeness was both "Him and "them" at the same time! (**vs. 27**)

Gen. 3:22

God again speaks within Himself
He speaks of Himself (singular) as "us" (plural)

Gen. 11:6, 7

God speaks again with Himself
He speaks again of Himself as "us" (**vs. 7**)

Psm. 2:7, 12

The Son is begotten of God
The Son has the attributes of God
(**Heb.1:4-12**) and is spoken to by God as God

Isa. 7:14

The Lord will give a sign – a Son to be born and called Immanuel (means God with us – (**Matt. 1:23**)
God sends God, by means of a virgin!

CHAPTER 2: WHO IS GOD?

Isa. 9:6, 7
>God's zeal will have a child born and a Son given
>The Son is called "the mighty God"

Isa. 6:8
>God speaks with Himself
>He calls Himself "us"
>Both concepts tied together – "***I send***" and "... ***go for Us***"

Isa. 48:16
>The "Spirit" is recognized as distinct and yet equal with the "Lord God"
>The doctrine of the Trinity is not exclusively a New Testament or Christian doctrine. It is clearly in the Old Testament which is foundational to ancient Judaism.

Matt. 3:16, 17
>Jesus' baptism brings all three members of the Trinity into action
>Each is distinct, separate, in agreement, and co-operating

John 14:16-36
>Jesus prays to the Father for the Holy Ghost to be sent (**vss. 16, 26**)
>Each is separate in function and inter-relationship
>Each member of the Trinity is to abide in the believers (**vss. 17, 20, 23**)

II Cor. 13:14
>Each of the Trinity has a separate ministry to believers
>We need all three ministering to us
>Any one area taken to an extreme at the neglect of others (taken intellectually, practically, emotionally, experientially, etc.) and apart from God's working, will end in disaster:

>*We end up as:*

>Hyper-Calvinists – trusting the grace of God and the doctrines of grace
>Liberals – over-emphasizing God's love and love for others
>Charismatic – trusting communion, gifts, and signs of the Spirit
>Rejection of the present ministry of one member of the Trinity is disastrous to our soul's health.

CHAPTER 3
GOD THE FATHER

SEPARATE PERSONHOOD AND TITLE

Matt. 28:19
Distinct from rest of Trinity in title.
To be so pictured in baptism.

I John 5:7
Distinct from rest of Trinity in heaven.
Bears His own witness apart from and yet in agreement with "**the Word**" and "**the Holy Ghost**."

John 14:16, 26
The Father is the receiver of Jesus' prayers.
He is the answerer by sending the Holy Ghost.

Titus 3:3-6
Called God our Saviour (**vs. 4**).
Saves us by the renewing of the Holy Ghost (**vs. 5**) through Jesus Christ (**vs. 6**).

I Cor. 15:24
Jesus will turn the Kingdom over to the Father.
This occurs after Jesus conquers all enemies including death (**vs. 26**).
This great event will thus occur after the millennium.

Eph. 2:13-18
Jesus reconciles us to God (the Father) (**vs. 16**) through the cross.
Through Jesus we have access by the Spirit to the Father.

I John 2:1
The Father (God) must be dealt with when we sin.
Jesus becomes our advocate before the Father.

I John 2:22, 23
Denial of the Father and the Son go together.
This is the mark of antichrist.
Denial of the Son means no possession of the Father.

Mark 1:10, 11
> The Father speaks from heaven "***My beloved Son.***"
> Jesus is being baptized and the Spirit descends here on earth at the same time.

Acts 10:38
> Act of "**God**" is distinct yet in full agreement with Jesus and the Holy Ghost.
> They also are called God elsewhere in the Bible.

FATHER OF THE SECOND MEMBER OF THE TRINITY

John 8:28, 29
> Jesus called Him Father (He never called Joseph father).
> Jesus spoke as taught by the Father.
> Jesus acted so as to please the Father.

John 17:1-5
> Jesus prayed to the Father by that title.
> Jesus claimed to be the Father's Son (**vs. 1**).
> Jesus finished the work given Him by the Father (**vs. 4**).
> Jesus received a people from the Father (**vs. 2**).
> Jesus had shared the Father's glory before there ever was a world (**vs. 5**).

Hebrews 1:1-2
> God speaks through Jesus the Son (**vs. 2**).
> God has made His Son "***heir of all things***" (**vs. 2**).

Hebrews 1:5-9
> Father has a relationship with the Son that He never had with angels (**vs. 5**).
> Son (pre-existed as Son as a begotten one) was brought into the world (**vs. 6**).
> Father and Son are both God (**vs. 8, 9).**

II Cor. 1:3, 4
> God is the Father of the Lord Jesus Christ.
> As the Father of Jesus, He is also the Father of Mercies and the God of all comfort.

CHAPTER 3: GOD THE FATHER

Gal. 4:4
>The Father sent the Son.
>The Father made use of a woman (Mary) that we might be redeemed.

John 3:16
>God has only one Son specially begotten.
>Father's love for us is seen by His sending of Jesus.

Matt. 8:29
>Even the demons recognize that Jesus is the Son of God – therefore that there is a Father.
>They recognize that the Father's rights of judgment have been given to the Son.

Eph. 1:3, 4
>As the Father of Jesus, He also is the blesser of the saved.
>Blessings are to all He has chosen.

Col. 1:19
>The Father of Jesus was pleased for all fullness to dwell in Jesus.
>The fullness of the Godhead can be seen bodily (**2:9**).

FATHER (SPIRITUAL) OF THE SAVED

Matt. 23:9
>God is the true Father of the Saved.
>No one else is to be given this title.
>It is reserved as special for God.

John 1:12, 13
>Our second birth is of God.
>We become sons of the Father.

Rom. 8:15-17
>Holy Spirit teaches us to say Father. ("**Abba**" is an intimate or family name for Father).
>Holy Spirit bears witness that we are the Sons of God.

I Pet. 1:3-5
>Father of Jesus has also begotten us.
>He keeps us to be revealed in the last time.

II Pet. 1:2-4

> The Father's power gives us all things.
> The Father gives us His nature through the promises.

John 20:17

> Jesus made it clear that His Father is also Father to us.
> We thus are of Christ's family.

I John 1:3

> We are to fellowship with the Father of Jesus.
> We fellowship as sons with a Father.

I John 3:1-3

> Father desires that we be called His sons!
> HE exercised and bestowed upon us a special manner of love.
> This relationship presently makes us so different from the world that they can't really know us.
> This relationship holds future benefits that are beyond anything we can now see.
> This relationship and future change cause us to purify ourselves.

II Cor. 6:17, 18

> God would be a Father to us in all of its benefits.
> He expects us to be separate from sin and the world (separated but not isolated or secluded).
> Lack of separation destroys benefits or our being Fathered by God. (Loss of blessing but not of relationship).

Contrast: John 8:44

> Lost have devil for their father.
> Devil's nature and works show themselves.

Matt. 13:38

> Tares are children of the wicked one.
> Satan's children often are lost religious people who actually appear rather good.

Eph. 2:2, 3

> Lost are called children of disobedience and children of wrath.
> This in contrast to those who have God as their Father.
> Two families of humanity – two fathers, two natures, two lifestyles.

CREATOR

(MENTIONED OVER 100 TIMES IN SCRIPTURE)

Gen. 1:1
God is the creator.
God pre-existed creation.
Time began at creation.

Neh. 9:6
Creator of all places.
Creator of all things.
Preserver of creation.

UNSEEN

Col. 1:15
Invisible to us.
Seen only in Jesus.

John 1:18
God has never been seen in His Person by human eye.
God by nature is unseeable.

John 14:7-9
Request to "see" the Father shows a misunderstanding of God's nature.
Jesus is the revelations given to help us.

INVOLVED IN OUR SALVATION

John 3:16
Father loved the world.
Love produced action of sending Jesus as a gift to us.
Father's love was to let us have everlasting life instead of perishing.

Gal. 4:4, 5
Father sent His Son.
Father acted according to a time schedule – when it was the "fullness."
Father had Son sent in human form
by virgin birth – "*made of a woman*"

by human race – "***under the law***"
Father sent Son:
to redeem
to make possible our adoption.

Isa. 53:6, 10, 11

Father laid our iniquity on Jesus.
Father bruised Jesus and put Him to grief (**vs. 10**).
Father made Jesus' soul an offering for sin.
Father's pleasure is prosper in Jesus' hand.
Father to see the travail of Jesus' soul and be satisfied. Thus, mercy and judgment can meet and a holy Father can justify the sinner! (**vs. 11**)

Col. 1:12-14

The Father made us able and qualified to be partakers of a wonderful inheritance – saints in light have it in common.
The Father delivered us from the power of darkness – Satan's Kingdom.
The Father charges and moves us into the Kingdom of His dear Son!

Heb. 9:14

Jesus offered Himself to the Father, without spot.
Jesus' blood purges our conscience so that we can serve the Father.

HAS A WILL

Eph. 1:11

The Father has a will of His own.
He can counsel with His will rather than be subject to the will of others.
He works out **all** things according to this counsel of **HIS** will.

Isa. 14:26, 27

God's will in purposes cannot be stopped.
God's will involves the whole earth and all nations – it is comprehensive
Prophecy is definite because He has thus revealed His will.

Isa. 46:9-11

There is no one else's will like the will of God.
God's will shall be done. His decisions shall be carried out.

CHAPTER 3: GOD THE FATHER

Dan. 4:35

God makes decisions that will stand not only for "***the inhabitants of the earth***" but also for "***the army of heaven***."
None, Satan included, can stop Him, or even challenge His actions.
Even a heathen King learned this and thus regained his sanity.

Rom. 8:28-31

God controls the end from the beginning in our salvation.
God guarantees the working together and result of all things in a believer's life.
Within God's will, there is surety and safety.

John 6:37

Father has given a group of people to Jesus.
All those given will come to Jesus.

II Thess. 2:13, 14

God has made a choice.
Choice involves salvation <u>through</u>
sanctification
belief of the truth
We enter this salvation as a result of being called by the Gospel.
Evidence of being chosen – having believed – having been called is the obtaining of the glory of our Lord Jesus Christ.

CHAPTER 4
GOD THE SON

THE LORD JESUS CHRIST

LORD
This is a title that refers to His deity, lordship, authority and power.

Rom. 14:9

Jesus' death had a goal, as well as His resurrection and ascension. Jesus was to be made LORD, both of the dead and the living.
To deny, avoid, reject, put off, or otherwise not submit to Jesus' Lordship is to deny in practice your confidence, benefit, or relationship to the work of Jesus, as well as His person and purpose.

I Cor. 12:3

The Holy Ghost does the work in our heart that not only produces the new birth, but also brings the confession of the Lord Jesus. (**Rom. 10:9a**).
Jesus is more than a potential Lord.
Jesus is more than a Lord.
Jesus is **THE LORD**.
Jesus will not share the throne with self or any other master. It is all or nothing.

Matt. 26:21-25

Judas' first exposure as a traitor was his inability to call Jesus, Lord. Master is close, but close will not do.
Jesus stated (vs. 25) that Judas had claimed the position of betrayer by what he said!
The issue of the Lordship of Christ is a test of Christ's work applied to us (Rom. 14), the work of the Holy Ghost in us (I Cor. 12), and the reality of our relationship to Him (Matt. 25).

Matt. 7:21-23

Many will call Jesus "Lord" when they have never entered into a vital relationship with Him.
These do many wonderful things without ever being truly saved.
These would seem to be the same many as are on the broad way (**vss. 13 and 14**).

The end of such is to be lost forever.
There is a difference between calling Jesus "Lord" as an empty formal title and knowing such with a submissive heart.

Isa. 43:11

Jesus alone has the right to be Lord.
Apart from His Lordship, there can be no salvation. There is no Saviour apart from being Lord also.

Isa. 33:22

A simple and practical definition of Lordship is here presented within the concept of being saved.

This is <u>not</u> to be separated into "a separate and after salvation experience" – (called different names by different groups, – saved and sanctified; first and second works of grace; entering the deeper life; salvation and discipleship; saved and dedicated, etc.)

Lordship can be broken into three areas: **<u>Judge</u>** or Judicial – He decides what is right and wrong. He judges our lives by His Word. He judges our past, present, and will one day judge us at the Judgment Seat of Christ.

<u>Lawgiver</u> or Legislative – He makes the laws by which we must live. We are to meditate in them day and night (**Psm. 1 and 2**), and

know them so well in our lives that we can teach others to "*observe all things whatsoever I have commanded you*" (**Matt. 28:20**).

<u>King</u> or Executive – He rules, enforcing the laws and protecting His followers. His is a Kingdom, and we are to be faithful and loyal citizens.

The three branches of Lordship cover the whole area of government. Literally, Jesus becomes our government – a loving but fully empowered dictator. We love Him and serve Him while He provides for us now and in the future.

JESUS

This is His NAME. It means Saviour, Deliverer, and is similar to the name "Joshua" of the Old Testament. This name has power, is disliked by Satan, is a channel for prayers, and is of great value to the believer (worthwhile to risk our life for it).

CHAPTER 4: GOD THE SON

Matt. 1:21
>This name was chosen by God and given to Joseph through the message of an angel.
>This name had particular meaning and revealed this purpose in coming to earth – <u>to save</u>.
>He was coming to save a particular people (His people).
>He would save the people <u>from</u> their sins. His name emphasizes more than a positional relationship. He is a Saviour that <u>SAVES</u>.

John 14:13-15
>Jesus' name is to be used in prayer.
>Use of His name (Jesus) results in His producing answers (**John 16:24**).

Consider also **Acts 16:18; Matt. 18:20; I Cor. 5:4; Acts 15:26,** etc.

CHRIST
This is a title that refers to Jesus' office as Messiah, the Promised One, and/or the Anointed One.

Matt. 24: 4, 5
>The term or title of Christ will be claimed by many in the Last Days.
>The claim of being an anointed minister, or promised one, or messiah to lead people to peace and prosperity, or combination of these will be self-proclaimed.
>Many will be deceived by these claims and follow such leaders (false Christs **vs. 24**).

John 1:20, 25
>Both John the Baptist and the Jewish leaders understood the meaning of the title, "Christ."
>John stated that he was preparing the way for the Christ (**vss. 25-29**).

John 4:24-26
>The Samaritan woman recognized the title "Christ" as belonging to the Messiah (**vs. 25**).
>Jesus claimed the title and office of both Messiah and Christ (**vs. 26**).

Matt. 16:16, 17

Peter's great confession involved recog-nizing Jesus as the Christ. This understanding is a result of revelation by God the Father.
One of our problems today is that we are attempting to accomplish by education and psychology what can only be accomplished by Divine revelation.

PRE-EXISTENCE

Jesus existed <u>before</u> His conception in Nazareth and birth in Bethlehem. The Bible teaching of Jesus' pre-existence and His deity are so close as to be nearly inseparable. If Jesus had not pre-existed His earthly life and ministry, He could not have been God.

Micah 5:2

Jesus was to be born in Bethlehem.
Even in 710 B.C. it could be said that His "***goings forth have been from of old***" – thus long before the prophecy.
Jesus' actions and thus existence was "***from everlasting***" or time without end into the past or eternity.

Isa. 9:6

While Jesus was a child born, He was also a son given (a son pre-existing but given through a child's birth).
Jesus is also called the <u>Everlasting</u> Father – thus one who lasts forever.

John 1:1-4

The "***Word***" is a descriptive title of Jesus.
He existed at the beginning as and with God.
He was not made because He was the maker of everything.

John 1:14, 15

The Word had pre-existed becoming flesh as He "was made flesh." Because this He was a spirit being.
Though He was made flesh, He did not permanently lose His glory, as was evidenced on the Mount of Transfiguration.
Although Jesus was born after John the Baptist (Luke 1:36, 57, 76), He existed before John.

John 8:56-59

Abraham (1900 B.C.) had seen Jesus' day.
Jesus existed as the "***I AM***" before Abraham.

CHAPTER 4: GOD THE SON

John 17:5
Jesus existed with His Father before the world existed (4004 B.C. approximately).
Jesus had shared the glory with the Father before creation.

Phil. 2:5-11
Jesus chose to humble Himself.
Involved in this humiliation is the taking on of a form of a servant and being made in the likeness of man.
His coming to earth as a man was preceded by an existence equal to and in the form of God (God is spirit). He has always been God but at a point in time, He also became man.

Col. 1:15-19
Jesus existed "**before all things**", therefore before birth and even creation.
He created **all** things and they were created **for Him**.

Rev. 1:8
Jesus is the very beginning (**Rev. 22:13**).
There could be nothing before Him. Thus, He existed long before His coming to earth as a man.

DEITY
Jesus is God. This is essential to the Christian faith. If He were not God, then He was a fraud, a liar, and deluded. Since He is and always has been God, we must submit, worship, and serve Him. Two terms must be separated for they are used differently by Modernistic teachers. Such would say they believe in the divinity of Jesus but not His deity. Modernists think of divinity as being unusual, above normal spiritually, and sometimes even god-like. This type of thinking is far short of Jesus' being actually and fully God (deity).

DIVINITY
D.D. degree – like God, of God, a clergyman – sacred, holy, supremely great.

Deity
is God, state of being a God.

IMPORTANCE

John 1:12

Salvation is tied to the person of Jesus; not His teaching, events, actions, etc.

Salvation is not tied to doctrine, church, decisions, altars, preachers, etc.

Who we receive that counts. All else is tied to His person, working, and our receiving.

I Cor. 15:17-19

Our hope is tied to Jesus.

If He is God. He can help us in the next life. If He wasn't, then we are without hope and **"most miserable."**

HIS CLAIMS

Luke 22:66-23:2

Jesus is quizzed as to whether He claimed to be the Christ.
He claimed even more, – that He was God the Son.
He claimed right to the titles of Son of man and Son of God.

John 10:30-33

Jesus claimed unity and sameness with God the Father.
Jesus' enemies understood His claim to being God.
Jesus did nothing to deny or change their statement about His being (claiming to be) God.

John 10:36-39

Jesus defended the thought that He was God.
Jesus used the title "Son of God" to claim His deity (term used 40 times in the N.T.).

John 14:7-11

Jesus made the claim of being God, this time to His disciples.
Jesus' claim of deity was given as a reason men should trust Him.
Jesus either told the truth (He is God) or was a liar and unworthy of any trust! If He is God, we must trust Him. Those who deny He is God cannot trust Him.

BIBLE TEACHING

Matt. 16:16, 17

CHAPTER 4: GOD THE SON

Peter declared that Jesus was God.
This was a result of the Father's revelation. Head knowledge is insufficient. We need God's heart revelation to see Jesus properly. That is why education, psychology, emotional pulls, etc. are insufficient in themselves to see men saved. Of course, entertainment, amusement, and fleshly programs won't do the job either.

Matt. 28:18-20

Jesus has all power.
Jesus can be with each believer anywhere, everywhere at once.
Such is possible only for God.
Jesus is given equal recognition with the Father and Holy Ghost in baptism. Such would be totally wrong except that Jesus is God.

Mark 2:5-11

Jesus not only healed but also forgave sins.
The power to forgive sins is for God only (**vs. 7**).

John 1:1-3

Jesus, the living Word, not only was with God, He also was God.
Jesus exercised the rights of deity by being the Creator.

John 17:1-3

Jesus is the dispenser of eternal life.
Eternal life is tied to knowing both Father and Son – (an equality in the Godhead.)

John 20:27-29

Thomas recognized that Jesus was resurrected from the dead.
He called Him, "**My Lord and my God**."
While deity and Lordship may be related, Thomas knew there was a difference.

Acts 3:12-15

Peter preached that Jesus was "**the Holy One**", the "**Just**", and "**the Prince of life**."
These terms are absolute as seen by "**the**" instead of "**a**."
Such could only be true of God.

Acts 7:57-60

Stephen prayed to Jesus as God.
Stephen knew Jesus as God and was honored by Him.

Rom. 9:1-5
Paul called Jesus "**God**."
Jesus is said to be "**over all**."

II Cor. 13:14
Jesus named with the Trinity.
First named and therefore not less than the Father and Holy Ghost.

Col. 1:13-19
Jesus has clear marks of deity given to Him.
Redemption of mankind (**vs. 14**).
Image of the invisible God (**vs. 15**).
Creator (**vs. 16**).
Maintainer and Preserver of all (**vs. 17**).
Has full pre-eminence (**vs. 18**).

Col. 2:8, 9
Christ contrasted with all philosophy, tradition of men, and thoughts of the world.
In Christ dwells "all the fulness of the Godhead bodily."

I Tim. 2:3-5
Jesus is the only mediator.
He is both God and man.

I Tim. 6:14-16
Jesus is given further titles of deity.
"Only Potentate"
"King of kings"
"Lord of lords"
"Who only hath immortality"
"Dwelling in the light which no man can approach unto."

II Tim. 4:1
Jesus will be the **Judge** of all – both saved and lost.
Jesus will have a future kingdom.

Titus 2:13
Jesus is called the "**great God**."
He is also called "**our Saviour**."

CHAPTER 4: GOD THE SON

Heb. 1:1-10

Jesus is heir of all things. No one else can interfere (**vs. 2**).
Jesus is the Creator.
Jesus is ...   the preserver of all things,
the Saviour from sin, and
now seated with glory (**vs. 3**).
Jesus is ...   above the angels, and
has a name above them (**vs. 4**).
Jesus received the worship of angels (**vs. 6**).
God the Father called Jesus God! (**vs. 8**).

Rev. 1:17, 18

Jesus is the first and the last; therefore, He is God.
Jesus as God controls both hell and death.
Jesus is resurrected from the dead and He will never die again.
Consider the following verses as they are excellent for dealing with Jehovah's Witnesses on this subject. Their twisted Bible still has enough truth left in it to show that Jesus is God:

Rev. 1:17:18 –

Jesus is called "the first and the last."

Isa. 44:6 –

The title "*first and last*" is here used for God alone (Jehovah). It states that besides "*the first and the last*" there is no God.

Isa. 48:11, 12 –

The One who is "*The first and the last*" will not share His glory with anyone else.

Isa. 41:4 –

A title for God (Jehovah) is "*The First One.*"

Rev.22:12-15 –

Three titles are given to Jesus:

- **"The First and the Last"**
- **"Alpha and Omega"**

– "The Beginning and the End"

Rev. 1:8 –

"**Alpha and Omega**" is a title for the LORD (Jehovah God) the Almighty. Therefore, Jesus is the Lord, God, the Almighty! This is taught even in the Jehovah's Witnesses own twisted Bible!

Generally, it is not safe or wise to use their "New World Translation" of the Bible as it has been re-written to promote their errors. However, in this case, God has let a warning witness slip past their revisers as light to show the honest that the Watch Tower Society teachings are wrong!

INCARNATION

by means of the Virgin Birth. Incarnation means that Jesus (pre-existence and deity) takes on human form and becomes both God and man.

Gen. 3:14, 15

Satan's defeat was to be through a human – not an angel or specially created being (**Heb. 2:9, 16-18**).
This was to be accomplished by the "*seed*" of the woman, not of man and woman.

Gal. 3:16

Christ was to come through Abraham.

Gen. 21:12 –

Christ was to come through Isaac.

Gen. 49:10 –

Christ was to come through Judah.

Acts 2:29, 30

Christ was to come through David.
The gap from Judah to David was 10 generations (**Matt. 1:3-6**) because of Pharez (**Gen. 38**) (**Deut. 23:2**).

CHAPTER 4: GOD THE SON

The coming of Christ through this line was according to the flesh (body), but not the spirit (He always has been a Spirit).

Psm. 69:7-9

This is an obvious prophecy regarding Jesus (**vs. 9 and John 2:17**).
His brethren are called "***my mother's children.***" (Contradicting Roman Catholic error of perpetual virginity of Mary).
Joseph obviously was not Jesus' father, though the father of Jesus' brethren.

Isa. 7:14

God is to give a "***sign***" to His people.
Special "***sign***" is that a "***virgin***" would conceive.
Result of miraculous conception will be a son, - even a greater biological miracle.
The name "***Immanuel***" means "**God with us.**"
The "***sign***" explains the miraculous means of God coming as a son through a virgin birth!

Isa. 9:6

The child is to be born, but the Son is given.
The Father thus gave the Son through a child being born.

Matt. 1:18-23

God here defines how Jesus was born.
Mary was with child, not of man, but of the Holy Ghost.
The Father used the Holy Ghost to prepare a body for the Son.
Mary stayed a virgin until after Jesus' birth (**vss. 24, 25**) to remove any doubt about Jesus' origin.

Luke 1:26-35, 46, 47

Luke was a medical doctor.
God had him record the medical details of the virgin birth.
What happened is explained in **Matthew**, but how it happened is explained here (**vss. 34, 35**).
Mary recognized Jesus as Saviour! (**vss. 46, 47**)
There could have been no immaculate conception. Mary had a Saviour and therefore recognized herself as a sinner.

John 1:14

"***The Word***" (a name for Jesus) was God (**vs. 1**).

"***The Word was made flesh***." God was made a human also!
"**Made**" implies a creative act.

John 3:13

"***Son of Man***" had His origin in heaven.
He had come down (to be lifted up like Moses' serpent) yet was still in heaven!

John 8:41

The Jews knew Jesus' birth was different.
They thought and accused Him of having been born illegitimately.
They couldn't grasp the truth of the virgin birth.

Gal. 4:4, 5

God sent Jesus.
"***His Son***" was a Son when sent, - He didn't become a son!
Jesus was "made of a woman."

Phil. 2:6, 7, 8

Jesus' coming involved being "***made***."
He was "***in the likeness of men,***" "***in fashion as a man***", yet without the sin nature of a man. In this alone He was different.

Col. 4:14

Luke was a doctor
He wrote the clearest record of the birth.
Luke had talked to eyewitnesses – (Mary was the only possible eyewitness to all that was involved in the virgin birth). – Luke also was given by God "***perfect understanding of all things from the very first***."
A court of law could not ask for a better witness on the subject of God becoming man.

I Tim. 3:16

A mystery to many – especially unbelievers.
God was manifest in the flesh.
Clear witnesses to this fact are listed.

Heb. 2:9

"Jesus, who was made."
Made a little lower than the angels.

Heb. 2:14
> Jesus was a partaker of "**flesh and blood**."
> He became like us in all ways.

Heb. 2:16-18
> "**Took on**" the seed of Abraham
> He identified with us fully.

I John 4:1-3
> "Jesus Christ is come in the flesh."
> The origin, process, and result are all important.
> This is the test of truth and error!

THE SINLESS LIFE OF JESUS
> If Jesus had sinned, He would have had to die for His own sins. He would not have been able to die for ours!

Isa. 53:9
> Jesus had "done no violence"
> Jesus never had "any deceit in His mouth."

I Pet. 2:22
> Jesus "did no sin."
> There was no "guile found in His mouth."

Matt. 27:3, 4
> Judas declared Jesus innocent.
> The Chief Priests and Elders did not argue the issue but said it was no issue to them!

Matt. 27:19
> Pilate's wife declared Jesus a "**Just man**."
> No one debated this issue.

Mark 1:23, 24
> An unclean spirit called Jesus holy – "**the Holy One of God**."
> This is not normal for demons as they normally are accusers.

Luke 9:29
> Jesus was transfigured while praying. (How about us?)
> Even His raiment was affected by the glory – white and glistering.

Luke 23:41, 27

Thief said He had "***done nothing amiss***."
Centurion said He was "***a righteous man***."
It is unusual for criminals and military officers to claim any one is totally free from sin.

John 1:4, 5

Jesus is the source of light.
Light is in direct contrast to darkness.

John 3:19-21

Light is contrasted with evil.
Thus Jesus is the opposite of sin or evil

John 8:12

Jesus is the light, it is His very nature.
We have the ability to live according to this light!

John 8:46

Jesus gave His enemies an opportunity to accuse Him of sin.
None had nor ever did accuse Him of sin.

John 14:30

Despite Satan's tempting Jesus in all areas, he never could find a place or handle to have on Jesus. He had nothing on Christ.
Sin gives Satan a handle on us.

John 18:38

Pilate said, "I find in Him no fault at all!"
Unusual for a politician to not be able to find either sin or fault in anyone – especially a potential competitor for public good will and support.
Unusual for a judge to not find any fault at all in an accused.

John 19:4-6

Pilate twice more states Jesus' sinlessness, publicly.
Pilate was a corrupt politician who ends up defending Jesus before an organized mob.

Acts 3:14

Peter called Jesus the Holy One and Just.

CHAPTER 4: GOD THE SON

The Jewish people had heard this often before (sinlessness of Jesus) and offer no argument against it.

Acts 4:27, 28

<u>Disciples</u> called Jesus the holy child.
This was in prayer to the Father and was honored with an answer.

II Cor. 5:20, 21

Jesus "knew no sin."
This is foundational to our being made right in God's eyes and even the righteousness of God.
If Jesus had sinned, there could have been no salvation for us. The whole basis of being our substitute is based on this fact.

Heb. 1:8, 9

Sceptre of Christ's Kingdom is a "***sceptre of righteousness***."
Jesus loved righteousness and hated iniquity. (You can't have one without the other).
God's anointing is evidence of Christ's righteous life and love of righteousness.

Heb. 4:15, 16

<u>Jesus was tempted</u> in all points – "*like as we are.*"
Jesus was "**without sin**."

Heb. 5:9

Jesus was made perfect.
This does <u>not</u> refer to sin removed and perfected.
This refers to completion in all areas due to sufferings (**vs. 8, 2:10**).

Heb. 7:26-28

Jesus didn't have to offer a sacrifice up for His own sins.
He was holy, harmless, undefiled, and separate from sins.

I Pet. 1:19

Jesus' blood was precious because He was sinless.
He was without blemish or spot.

I Pet. 2:21-24

Jesus did no sin.
No guile was found in His mouth.
He never responded to sin in like kind.

I Pet. 3:18
>We are called unjust because we are sinners.
>Jesus is called just because He was sinless.

I John 1:5

There was no darkness in God.

I John 3:3

Jesus is pure; therefore we should purify our-selves.

I John 3:5

In Jesus is no sin!

SUBSTITUTIONARY DEATH
>A central theme of the Bible and History.
>Death described at length twice in the O.T. (**Psm. 22 and Isa. 53**) and four times in the N.T. (each Gospel), plus being mentioned multitudes of other places.

Gen. 2:17
>Sin brings death.
>The death shows in various forms: spiritual, social, environmental, economical, and eventually physical.
>**Rom. 6:23** – this principle still operates.

Gen. 3:21
>Mankind's sin caused the death of an animal – to obtain the skins.
>Type or example of sacrifice was here established.

Gen. 4:1-5
>Abel chose an occupation to fit himself for service, sacrifice, faith, obedience, and meditation. Cain chose otherwise.
>Abel operated by faith (**Heb. 11:4**), therefore acting on God's command.
>Both must have known that animal sacrifice (blood and death) was required.
>Cain chose fruit to offer (no blood or death) and was rejected.

Gen. 22:7, 8
>Isaac understood the principle of sacrifice.
>Great prophecy, – God to provide Himself a lamb – a sacrifice – a burnt offering.

CHAPTER 4: GOD THE SON

Exodus 11
> teaches of the Passover sacrifice.

Leviticus
> teaches of many sacrifices to be made.

Psm. 22:1, 7, 8
> David prophesied of Jesus' death.
> Quotes from the cross were given over 1000 years <u>before</u> the event!

Psm. 22:14-18
> Details of Jesus' crucifixion in events and suffering recorded ahead of time!
> God was focusing attention to this event 10 centuries before it happened!

Psm. 69:7-9
> Our reproaches were put on Jesus ... He became our substitute.
> **Rom. 15:3** records the fulfillment of this prophecy.

Isa. 52:13; 53:12
> This is perhaps the clearest picture of Jesus' suffering.
> He was marred for many nations (**52:13, 14**).
> He bore our griefs and carried our sorrows (**53:4**)
> He was wounded for our transgressions, He was bruised for our iniquities, the chastisement of our peace was upon Him (**53:3**).
> Father laid on Jesus our iniquities (**53:6**).
> He was stricken for the transgression of others (**53:8**).
> He (sinless) had His soul made an offering for sin (ours) (**53:10**).
> He bore our iniquities (**53:11**).
> He bare the sin of many (**53:12**).
> All this is how Jesus was our substitute in His death!

Zech. 13:6
> Future – therefore prophecy.
> Jesus still has wounds, for He has given His blood which would be needed to heal them.

Matt. 16:21-23
> Jesus taught His death ahead of time.
> Satan, through Peter, resisted the teaching of a planned ("must") death.

Luke 9:30, 31

Jesus' death was the topic of discussion on the Mount of Transfiguration.

Jesus' death was to be an accomplishment! ... Not a defeat, circumstance, event etc.

Moses and Elijah, representing the Law and the Prophets, saw Jesus' death as the focus of Jesus' coming!

Luke 24:25-27

Jesus talked with two disciples on the way to Emmaus on the need for suffering to precede glory.

The Law and the Prophets were clear on this subject.

John 10:11

Jesus' is the good shepherd.

Jesus was to be the substitute for the sheep.

John 10:17, 18

Jesus was to lay His life down.

No one took Jesus' life, – He gave it as a willing sacrifice.

John 12:23, 24

Jesus expected to be glorified through dying.

Death brings fruit, and the saved are the fruit of His death. (Fruit takes on or shows the nature of the seed).

John 12:31-33

Satan considered Jesus death was a "great victory" of Satan, but "death" was swallowed up in victory (1 Corinthians 15:54-57) (a defeat for Satan).

His death also has drawing power to mankind.

People blame Pilate, Herod, Caiaphas, Jewish leaders, Romans, Satan, and/or demons etc... **BUT** Jesus laid down His life for ungodly rebels that we might be saved!

I Cor. 2:8

Satan is the "prince of the power of the air" (Eph. 2:2), "prince of the devils" (Matt. 12:24), or "prince of this world" (John 12:31).

Eph. 6:12 makes it clear that Satan's Kingdom includes rulers and principalities of this world system.

Satan and his workers brought on the crucifixion and defeat through his (and their) ignorance.

CHAPTER 4: GOD THE SON

Acts 2:22-24
God's counsel and foreknowledge delivered up Jesus to die.
Mankind was willing and desirous of taking Jesus and crucifying Him.
It was previously decided that Jesus would die (**Rev. 13:8**) and only waited time for it to be accomplished.

Rom. 4:24, 25
Jesus' death was based on His being <u>delivered</u> to it (by God) not taken away from God.
His death was:
<u>for</u>   – a positive action
<u>our</u>   – a personal action
<u>offences</u>   – a practical action

We had offended God by sin. Yet, God delivered up His only begotten Son to suffer what we deserved.

Rom. 5:6-8
We had no strength by which to save ourselves.
Christ died <u>for us</u> (**vs. 8**).
We were ungodly (**vs. 6**) and sinners (**vs. 8**). These are the only kinds of people Jesus died for.

Rom. 8:31, 32
The Father delivered up Jesus <u>for us</u>!
There is nothing of greater value; now He <u>freely</u> gives us <u>all</u> things!

I Cor. 5:7
Christ is the Passover Lamb. He provides protection from judgment.
He was sacrificed <u>for us</u>.
His death was a substitute for ours.

I Cor. 6:20
Saved are bought with a price.
He now owns us because of His becoming our substitute.

I Cor.15:3, 4
Christ died for <u>our sins</u> and this was done according to the Scriptures.
The substitutionary death of Jesus is the beginning of the Gospel.

Gal. 3:13, 14
> We were under the curse of the law.
> Jesus was "***made a curse <u>for us</u>***", by means of His substitutionary death.
> Now instead of a curse we get both a blessing and a promise.

Gal. 4:4, 5
> Jesus came to redeem us.
> The result for us is we are adopted as sons.

Heb. 2:9, 14-18
> Jesus became man to die for men.
> For His death to be substitutionary and make reconciliation for sins, He had "***to be made like unto His brethren***."

Heb. 9:25-28
> Jesus died <u>once</u> for us.
> Mass with its transubstantiation (re-sacrifice of Jesus) is impossible and un-Biblical.

I Pet. 1:10-12
> The clear understanding of the substitu-tionary death was not grasped by the prophets nor by angels.
> Preaching of the Gospel brings under-standing beyond the facts.

I Pet. 1:18-20
> Jesus' death involved His <u>blood</u>.
> This is the foundation of our salvation.

I Pet. 2:24
> Jesus as a substitute, <u>bore our sins</u> in His own body.
> His stripes produced spiritual healing so that we can now live unto righteousness. It is <u>far better</u> to be able to live holy than just be healthy

I Pet. 3:18
> Jesus was just while we were unjust.
> He took our place, the just for the unjust, when He suffered for sins.

I John 2:2
> "***Propitiation***" means to appease the wrath of the one who has been offended ... to pacify.
> Jesus took our place to pacify the wrath of God against sin.

CHAPTER 4: GOD THE SON

Rev. 5:8-12

Jesus' actions in dying as a substitute qualify Him as the "**Worthy**" One.
He should receive the praise for providing such a salvation.

Rev. 13:8

By agreement and covenant, Jesus was "the Lamb slain from the foundation of the world."
He accomplished it in fact and time on Mt. Calvary over 1900 years ago.
What has He determined that we need to accomplish?

JESUS' BLOOD – THE WORK IT DOES

Denial of Christ's blood's working is a great heresy. Contrast the errors of Liberalism, Jehovah's Witnesses, Mormons, Theism, John McArthur, and others to what the **BIBLE** teaches.
In most all cases, it is not the existence of blood but two greater issues:
The emphasis put on the blood of Jesus, and
What work we say the blood actually does.

Acts 20:28

Jesus' blood purchased the local Church.
A true Church has been bought and is not its own, nor does it belong to its members etc.
The Holy Ghost qualifies, selects, and places overseers in the Church.

Rom. 5:8, 9

Jesus' blood justifies us.
Jesus' blood makes it so that we can be saved from wrath.
His blood went beyond what His death did – "***Much more then***."

I Cor. 10:16

Jesus' blood provides for a Communion.
His body suffered; therefore, there is the fellowship of His sufferings (**Phil. 3:10**).
His blood was poured out; therefore, we can have the fellowship of sacrifice!

Eph. 1:7

Jesus' blood gives forgiveness of sins.

Individual sins were cared for, not just sin in general or the sin nature.
The Old Testament sacrifices only covered sins, but Jesus' blood gives forgiveness!

Eph. 2:8-13

Jesus' blood brings us near to God.
Gentiles as well as Jews are brought close.

Col. 1:20

Jesus' blood made <u>peace with God</u>.
This is the basis of our being reconciled to God.

Heb. 9:12

Jesus' blood obtained <u>eternal redemption</u> for us.
Jesus' blood is superior to animal blood.

Heb. 9:14

Jesus' blood <u>purges our conscience</u>. It cleans away the stain, removes the sin, and makes our conscience without blemish!
This takes us "***from dead works***" so that we can "***serve the living God***."

Heb. 10:19

Jesus' blood gives us access "***into the holiest***" or throne room of God.
Boldness to enter is now ours.
A ministry of prayer is provided.

Heb. 13:12

Jesus' blood purchased <u>our sanctification</u>.
Holy living is now possible.
Usefulness is now available to us.
Separation and dedication are now provided for each of us.
Justification has to do with salvation from the <u>penalty</u> of sin, while sanctification deals with salvation from the <u>power</u> of sin.
We don't have to work up to this, agonize it down, or earn it. Jesus paid for it with His blood. We should enter into it and enjoy it in practice.

Heb. 13:20

Jesus' blood provided the <u>Everlasting Covenant</u>.
This covenant has no end.

CHAPTER 4: GOD THE SON

This blood works great results: i.e. **vs. 21**:
"make you perfect"
"every good work"
"do His will"
"working in you."

I Pet. 1:2

Jesus' blood has continual use after salvation.
Matches up with our obedience.
Sprinkling speaks of efficiency as well as O.T. types in sacrifices.
This "***sprinkling***" has to do with Jesus' blood, and is in <u>no</u> way connected to a form of baptism (dipping and dying).

I John 1:7

Jesus' blood cleanses from sin.
It actually removes the sin from us. There is deliverance.
– See **Rev. 1:5** also.

I John 5:8

Jesus' blood <u>bears witness</u> in us, – to us and to others.
II Cor. 4:7 "We have this treasure in earthen vessels."

Rev. 5:9

Jesus' blood works in all kindreds and nations.
It is not just for Jewish people nor any other single national or racial groups. It is available to all!

Rev. 12:11

Jesus' blood <u>defeats Satan</u>.
This will explain the devil's hatred of this subject.

Acts 5:28

Jesus' blood condemns the lost.
Rejecting Jesus makes one guilty of that blood – blood guiltiness.
Matt. 27:24, 25 – One's attitude toward Jesus is identical to His attitude toward the blood.

Heb. 10:29

Jesus' blood brings <u>judgment/punishment</u> to those who count it less than holy.
This is as bad as despising the Holy Spirit and walking over Jesus.

Rom. 3:25

Jesus' blood was how He became <u>our propitiation.</u>
This is realized through faith in His blood.

Heb. 12:24

Jesus' blood <u>speaks</u>.
This is more than poetical terminology. It actually has "things" to say – better than what Abel's blood said (**Gen. 4:10**).

Rev. 7:14

Jesus' blood washed robes white.
Righteous living (**Rev. 19:7, 8**) is made possible through the blood.

Thus we see 21 different things that Jesus' blood does! There are probably others that you can locate and add to this list. We must stand without compromise against those heretics who would ignore or devalue Jesus' blood. It is "***holy***" blood, God's blood, pure blood, working blood. The Bible states that "***without shedding of blood is no remission.***" (**Heb. 9:22b**).

Matt. 27:4 – Teaches that Jesus' blood was "*innocent blood*." No guilt could there be found. In this, it is different from any human blood.

Acts 20:28 and I John 1:7

These verses make it clear that Jesus' blood was God's blood! Thus it is unique and lasting blood. It is not subject to the laws of science in make-up, endurance, or usefulness. It is far superior to human blood. God would not accept human blood in the Old Testament for a sacrifice because it was tainted by the Fall. He took animal blood (untainted) as a covering. But Jesus' blood is even higher (**Heb. 9:12**).

I Pet. 1:19

Jesus' blood is "***precious blood***." It was precious to God the Father who accepted it; it was precious to the Son who shed it; and it was precious to the Holy Spirit who helped offer it. How precious is Jesus' blood to you? In what ways is it precious?

JESUS' BURIAL

- Death is not the end of existence; it is a change of spheres.
- Death to the physical world brings a time of spiritual warfare.

CHAPTER 4: GOD THE SON

I Cor. 15:1-4

Christ's burial is the second part of the Gospel – the most neglected part.
We are to fully identify with the Gospel, – receive, stand in, and keep in memory.
Christ's burial pictures sanctification.
We are to be buried with Him.

Rom. 6:1-6

Believers <u>have been</u> buried with Jesus
(vs. 4).
Water baptism pictures our salvation.
This is <u>not water baptism</u> but salvation
(vss. 2, 3, 4, 5).
Salvation involves a burial that frees us so that we no longer need to serve sin (**vs. 6**).
Water baptism pictures His and our death, burial, and resurrection.
Only immersion can picture the true gospel. It is an outward sign of what has been experienced within the soul.
Jesus' burial is quite important. What happened during that time teaches us more about the Biblical Gospel of our salvation.

Matt. 12:38-40

Jonah is a picture of Jesus.
Both were to have a 3-day and 3-night experience.
Jonah spent his "in the whale's belly."
Jesus was to spend His "**in the heart of the earth**" (center not surface).
The body was in the tomb but He was in the center of the earth.

Eph. 4:7-11

Jesus had to descend first into the lower parts of the earth (different from a tomb).
When He later "**ascended up on high**" He
"led captivity captive"
"gave gifts unto men."

Luke 16:19-26

Jesus taught that hell and Abraham's bosom were close together.
Heaven wasn't promised to O.T. saints or even the thief on the cross.

Abraham's bosom was a place of rest and comfort – seemingly Paradise (**Luke 23:43**).

Col. 2:14, 15

Jesus "spoiled principalities and powers."
This involved defeating them <u>and</u> taking of their goods (spoils). (**Mark 3:27; Isa. 14:17**).
When we enter into His burial, we obtain of His victory and the freeing of captives.
Jesus accomplished this openly and so should we.

Col. 2:12, 13

Our new life (quickened) and our forgiveness is a result of being "***risen with Him***."
Before the resurrection with Him we are first "***buried with Him***."
Our burial is first for our salvation and then ongoing for victory.
Burial involves separation from the world and free operating in the spiritual realm.

Heb. 2:14, 15

Jesus has <u>already</u> defeated Satan.
Satan <u>had</u> the power of death but lost it to Jesus who now controls the keys (**Rev. 1:18**).
We no longer have to fear death.
The way to victory is to follow Jesus as our example (**Rev. 12:11**).

Gen. 22:8

Great prophecy of Jesus presents Him as God's Lamb (**John 1:29**).
Jesus is prophesied to become a <u>burnt</u> offering.
Many of the sacrificial types of Christ in the Old Testament were to be burnt by fire.

Psm. 16:10

Here David gives a prophecy of Jesus to be resurrected.
It is clear that Jesus was to go to hell but not to stay there.

Acts 2:25-31

Peter preached on the day of Pentecost that Jesus had fulfilled David's prophecy.
Issue was <u>not</u> the location of Jesus' body (in the tomb), but of His soul (in hell) thus becoming a <u>burnt</u> offering.
The resurrection guaranteed the end of Christ's possible time in hell.

Therefore Jesus went to hell while in the heart of the earth (**Matt. 12:38-40**). This locates physically the place called Hell.

Luke 23:43

Jesus promised the thief on the cross that they would be together in Paradise that same day.

Thus we learn that Paradise was located (then) in the heart of the earth (**Matt. 12:38-40**). It now is relocated to the third heaven (**II Cor. 12:1-4**). "*When He ascended up on high, He led captivity captive,*" (**Eph. 4:8**).

I Pet. 3:18-20

Jesus used time between death and resurrection (burial time) to preach to "*spirits in prison.*"

These "*spirits*" were of those who were disobedient before the flood ... while the ark was being built. This is quite specific and cannot be stretched to mean a second chance for the lost. The time period (perhaps 120-years) compared to perhaps 4035 years of time indicates only 3 percent of the total time period.

Preaching does not necessarily imply a Gospel invitation. It may involve further condemnation (**Isa. 6:9-11**).

These spirits might have been the ungodly (**II Pet. 2:5**) who were judged and/or the disobedient angels (**Jude 6; Gen. 6:1-4**), who left and are reserved for judgment. They obviously are not free spirits.

Burial with Christ should make heaven, hell, and the definite judgment of the lost real to us.

Heb. 9:12, 23-28

Jesus took His blood to heaven for us.

This was at His ascension following His descension (**Eph. 4:7-9**) ... not the public ascension from the Mount of Olives 40-days after the resurrection. This occurred shortly after the resurrection.

– John 20:17, 18 – Jesus asked not to be touched as He hadn't yet ascended.

– Matt. 28:9 – A short time later Jesus allowed Himself to be touched and held.

– John 20:27 – Jesus now invites Thomas to touch Him.

Mark 14:3-9

Mary's anointing (**John 12:1-8**) of Jesus was to prepare His "***body***" for burial.

This event is to be spoken of wherever the **GOSPEL** is preached in the whole world (**Matt. 26:13**).

The Bible makes special note of the care of Jesus' body for the burial time.

Matt. 27:58 – Joseph begs for Jesus' body.

Matt. 27:59 – It is wrapped in a clean linen cloth.

Matt. 27:60 – It is put in a new tomb; one of Joseph's own making.

John 19:38-42 – Nicodemus assisted in the burial. Myrrh and aloes (spices) were used to preserve the body ... 100 lbs. weight.

John 20:6, 7 – The body was wound in linen clothes (**19:40**) with a separate napkin for around His head.

Luke 23:55, 56 – Women had observed at least the first part of the body's preparation. They also gathered spices and ointments for His body.

Mark 16:1-5 – They came very early on the <u>first day of the week</u> to anoint the body of Jesus.

Great honor was given to Jesus by the care given to His body. It was not burned, tossed aside, neglected, rejected, or considered of little or no value. There should be a lesson in this for us.

Luke 23:46

Jesus gave His spirit to God the Father.

This act was in line with the prophecy of **Psm. 31:5.**

Stephen followed somewhat the same pattern in **Acts 7:59**.

This is all according to the teaching of **Eccl. 12:7:** body to dust to the earth, the spirit returned to God.

We are given a body and a spirit with which we are to glorify God (**I Cor. 6:19, 20**). We are a soul or ... a soul is what we really are.

Jesus' burial pictures clearly these three areas:

He (soul) went to the heart of the earth (but God wouldn't leave Him there – His soul that is - **Acts 2:25-31**).

His Spirit returned to heaven.

His Body was laid in the grave.

JESUS' RESURRECTION

Christ's resurrection is one of the clearest proved facts in history.

This sets Christianity apart from all other religions.

If there had been no physical bodily resurrection, it would have meant that Jesus was not God.

CHAPTER 4: GOD THE SON

I Cor. 15:1-4

The resurrection is a part of the message of the saving gospel.
There could have been no real salvation in a dead Saviour.
A true Saviour must overcome death and hell to bring us real life and resurrection if heaven is to become ours.
The resurrection was according to the Scriptures.

I Cor. 15:5-8

There were clear evidences of the resurrection.
Jesus was seen many times, six of which are recorded here:

Peter (Luke 24:34)	James
Twelve	All the apostles
500	Paul

A study of the rest of the New Testament would allow you to add many other sightings to this list.

Acts 1:1-3

Jesus showed Himself alive.
He used many infallible proofs.
He was seen over a period of 40-days.
This certainly was much too long to be a dream or a vision.

John 20:14-20

Mary Magdalene saw Jesus and talked with Him.
The ten disciples (**vs. 24**) saw Jesus, His hands and side, and heard Him speak. They were changed from fear to gladness.

John 20:26-29

Jesus was seen of the disciples (11) with Thomas present.
Offer made to be touched and the open side could be reached into.
Thomas changed from doubt to belief.

John 21:1, 9-14

Jesus here appears a third time to the disciples (**vs. 14**).
Jesus fed the disciples, – hardly the act of a bodiless spirit.

Luke 24:13-16, 30

Jesus appeared to two disciples on the road to Emmaus.
He took, held, and broke bread.

He blessed a meal but seemingly did not eat it.
He had the ability to vanish in His resurrected body.

Luke 24:36-45

Disciples mistakenly thought Jesus was a spirit.
Jesus shows His hands and feet, offers to be handled, and makes clear He has a physical body.
His body is described as flesh and bones as the blood was already in heaven.
He ate both fish and honeycomb.

Acts 1:3-11

This would be the fourth appearance (at least) of Jesus to the disciples.
This time they were comfortable with Him and discussing the future.

Acts 2:22-24

The "**Resurrection**" was a definite part of Peter's message.
The resurrection produced boldness in Peter he didn't have before Christ's death.
It is a curious fact that the Roman Catholic Church, that makes so much over Peter, leaves out the resurrection in the Stations of the Cross, etc.!

Acts 20:7

The "**Resurrection**" brought a change in the day of worship, fellowship, and preaching.
By this point the first day of the week had become the normal day of meeting.
I Cor. 16:2 shows that this was the day the believers cared for their giving to missionary work etc.

Rev. 1:18

Jesus stated to John that He was resurrected.
The Bible records Jesus' claim.

Matt. 28:5, 6

An angel declared Jesus was risen.
He offered the proof of an empty grave.

Luke 24:12

Peter saw the empty linen clothes that had before been wrapped around the body of Jesus.

CHAPTER 4: GOD THE SON

Peter had to face evidence that Jesus wasn't dead.

John 20:9

The Scriptures required a resurrection (**Luke 24:23-27**).
Often we don't understand clearly Scriptural prophecies until after their fulfillment.

I Cor. 15:12-19

The resurrection was a necessity if there was to be a real salvation. Without a resurrection we are a miserable people.

I Cor. 15:20-23

The resurrection guarantees victory over the results of Adam's sin. Our race was condemned without hope due to Adam. Jesus reversed this. Now it is a personal relationship that must be entered into for our personal situation

RESULTS OF JESUS' RESURRECTION

Acts 13:26-38

It is a theme in the message of salvation.
It was a fulfillment of prophecy.

Acts 17:30-32

It is the guarantee of righteous judgment.

Rom. 1:4

It gives proof of the deity of Jesus.

Rom. 4:24, 25

It provided our justification.

Rom. 7:4

It makes possible our bearing of fruit.

Rom. 14:9

It gives Jesus rights to full Lordship over mankind.

I Cor. 15:22

It produces life for those "*in Christ*."

II Cor. 4:14

It guarantees our resurrection.

Eph. 1:19, 20
    It showed the great power that now operates in the saved.

Col. 3:1
    It has us seeking heavenly things.

Heb. 7:25
    Jesus is now our intercessor (also mediator and advocate).

I Pet. 1:3, 4
    It gives us a lively hope.

Rev. 1:18
    He now controls the keys of hell and death.

Acts 20:7 etc.
    It brought a change in the day of worship.

John 16:7 (20:22 and Acts 2)
    It made possible the sending of the Holy Spirit to His present ministry in and for us.

ASCENSION OF CHRIST

Mark 16:19, 20
    "<u>Received</u> up into heaven" by
    – God the Father
    – Elect Angels
    – Old Testament Saints
    "<u>Sat</u> on the right hand of God."

Luke 24:49-53
    "<u>Carried</u> up into heaven"
    – By whom? Father? Holy Spirit?
    Heaven is where He came from (**John 17:4, 5**), and where He returned.

Acts 1:6-11
    "Taken up"
    To return "in like manner"

Acts 7:54-59
    Jesus stands to receive the first martyr.

Seen also by Saul/Paul (**I Cor. 9:1; 15:8**), Ananias (**Acts 9:10, 17**) and John (**Rev. 1**).

JESUS' PRESENT MINISTRY

John 14:16

He sent the Holy Spirit for particular and special ministries.
John 16:7 – The Holy Spirit is able to continue Christ's personal ministries to our benefit.

John 14:20

Christ indwells the believer.
This is the basis of successful Christian living (**Gal. 2:20**).

Matt. 16:18

Christ <u>builds</u> the Church.
Christ <u>owns</u> the Church.
That which is built of man and/or owned by men is <u>not</u> Christ's nor can it truly be called a Church.

Rom. 8:34

Christ intercedes for us.
His intercession makes for a full salvation (**Heb. 7:25**).
Makes intercession for the lost to be saved (**Heb. 7:25**).

Rom. 8:35

Jesus loves us.
Nothing can separate us from His love.

Eph. 1:22, 23

He is the head of the Church.
His headship is in <u>all</u> areas.
We are the body to respond to His mind.

Eph. 4:7-11

He gives gifts to men.
He gives gifted men to the Church.
He decides which church gets which of His gifted men.

Eph. 5:25-27

He sanctifies and cleanses us.
He desires and works to make us a glorious Church, holy, without blemish, spot or wrinkle!

(**John 13**) The ordinance of foot washing was to remind us of this.
(**Heb. 2:11**) Because He sanctifies us, He is not ashamed to call us "***Brethren***"!

I Tim. 2:5

He is a mediator.
The only mediator between God and man as He is both God and man!
(Heb. 8:6) He mediates "*a better covenant.*"
(**Heb. 9:15**) He mediates "***the new testament.***" We therefore get an eternal inheritance.

Heb. 2:18

He helps and strengthens us when we are tempted.
His own experience prepared Him for this.
Temptation is a form of suffering to a holy person.

Heb. 2:17

He serves as our High Priest.
(**Heb. 4:14**) This should encourage us to hold fast.

I Pet. 2:25

Shepherd of our souls (**5:4** Chief Shepherd).
Bishop of our souls (Pastors are the ministers of the Bishop.)

I John 1:3-7

He desires to fellowship with us.
(**Rev. 3:20**) In the last days the church, in general, will operate without fellowshipping with Jesus.

I John 2:1

He is our advocate (legal representative) when we sin.
This should encourage us not to sin.

Jude 1

He preserves His saints.
He can keep us from falling and present us faultless! (**vss. 24, 25**).

Rev. 4:11

He still creates things for His pleasure.
(**Heb. 1:3**) He upholds all things by His power.
(**Col. 1:17**) He keeps all things together. They consist by His power.

CHAPTER 5
GOD THE HOLY SPIRIT

PERSONALITY – HE IS A PERSON

There is much confusion about the Holy Spirit and the issue of His being a person is important. He is not a force, influence, feeling, nor our conscience. He is as much a person as God the Father and God the Son. He has a personality with which the Bible Believing Christian should be familiar.

PERSONAL TRAITS

I Cor. 2:10

    Reveals truths to believers on behalf of the Father.
    Searches out matters – even the deep things of God.

I Cor. 2:11

    Has knowledge of God.
    Man can only access this knowledge through the Holy Spirit.

I Cor. 12:11

    Distributes spiritual gifts by <u>His working</u>.
    Gives these gifts according to <u>His will</u>.

Rom. 15:30

    Shows love.
    Should be loved.

Rom. 8:27

    Has a mind.
    Makes intercession.

PERSONAL ACTIONS

I Tim. 4:1

    Speaks.
    Warns of dangers.

Rev. 2:7

    Talks to churches.
    Heard by those with spiritual hearing.

Luke 12:12
Teaches us.
Ignoring Him leaves us saying wrong things.

John 14:26
He brings things to our remembrance.
We can't remember what we never learned.

Acts 13:2
He <u>calls</u> laborers to new areas of opportunity.
He <u>informs</u> churches of those whom He has called.

Rom. 8:26
He <u>helps</u> our infirmities.
He <u>prays</u> or makes intercession for us.

Rom. 8:14
He <u>leads</u> all those who are saved.
Are we following His leading?

RECEIVES PERSONAL TREATMENT

Matt. 12:31, 32
He can be <u>blasphemed</u>.
This is not true of feelings, impersonal forces, or power.

Acts 5:3
He can be <u>lied to</u>.
This was done by Ananias and Sapphira trying to appear more spiritual, more dedicated, and more sacrificial to the Church than they actually were.

Acts 5:9
He can be <u>tempted</u>.
Trying to appear more than we are tempts the Holy Spirit to send judgment.

Acts 7:51
He can be <u>resisted</u>.
Rejection of God's messengers is an act against the Holy Spirit.

Heb. 10:29
He can be <u>despised</u> and done despite to.

CHAPTER 5: GOD THE HOLY SPIRIT

He is not to be ignored, neglected, rejected, nor undervalued
He is not to be treated as inferior, a failure, nor the object of spite.

Eph. 4:30

He can be <u>grieved</u>.
This speaks of striking at the emotions of the Holy Spirit.

I Thess. 5:19

He can be <u>quenched</u>.
Though He has power enough, He can be offended till He withdraws from acting.

ASSOCIATED WITH THE OTHER TWO PERSONS OF THE GODHEAD

Matt. 28:19

He is given an equal position and pre-eminence.
Baptism is used to picture the three personalities but one God.

II Cor. 13:14

His ministries are given equal importance with the others.
The Apostolic benediction reminds us of equality of each.

I John 5:7

In Heaven they continue their equality and oneness.
They each bear record of our conversion!

PERSONAL CHARACTERS AND OFFICES

John 14:26

He is called the <u>Comforter</u>.
As a person, He comforts us.

I Cor. 6:11

He is called "the Spirit of our God."
He is the main operator on earth at this time on behalf of the Trinity.
He washes, sanctifies, and justifies in the name of the Lord Jesus.

Heb. 10:15

He is a witness to us.
We should accept His testimony.
He tells us of our relationship, with the Father (**Rom. 8:16**).

John 14:16
The Holy Spirit is called "He."
This is the same pronoun as that given to the Father.

John 14:26
Again the pronoun "He" is used.
This is in parallel with the pronoun "I" used for Jesus.

John 16:7
Here He is called "Him."
He will carry on the same work that Jesus started.

HIS DEITY – THE HOLY SPIRIT IS GOD!

HE IS CALLED GOD.

II Cor. 3:17, 18
He is called "Lord."
This is a title for God.

Acts 5:3, 4
The lie was not so much to the Church as to the Holy Ghost or God.
Peter recognized the Holy Ghost as God.

I Cor. 3:16, 17
Our bodies are three times called "**the temple of God**."
The temple is so named because it is indwelt by the Holy Spirit.

I Cor. 12:4-6
The variety of gifts for functioning are given by the Holy Spirit.
He is called "the same Spirit", "the same Lord", and "the same God."

HE HAS DIVINE ATTRIBUTES.

Rom. 1:4
He is called the "***Spirit of Holiness***."
Holiness is the leading attribute of God.

Heb. 9:14
He is called the "***Eternal Spirit***."
Eternity is time without either beginning or end. Only God is eternal.

CHAPTER 5: GOD THE HOLY SPIRIT

Psm. 139:7-10
The Holy Spirit is present (He exists) everywhere at once.
<u>Omnipresence</u> is possible only for God.

Luke 1:35
The Holy Ghost is said to have the "***Power of the Highest***."
There is no limit to His power, He is omnipotent.

I Cor. 2:10-11
The Holy Spirit has complete or all knowledge.
<u>Omniscience</u> is an attribute of God.

HE HAS DONE WORKS.

Job 26:13; 33:4
He was involved in creation.
The Father thought it, the Son spoke it, and the Spirit did it.

II Pet. 1:21
Inspiration or the Authoring of the Scriptures was an act of the Holy Ghost.
Inspiration is an act of God (**II Tim. 3:16**).

Matt. 1:20
The body for Jesus was the result of a special creative act of the Holy Ghost.
The Virgin Birth was His miraculous act.

Matt. 12:28
Jesus as God could have cast out demons in His own power.
Jesus chose to use the same means we would have as citizens of the Kingdom of God.
The Holy Spirit has power over demons and all of Satan's Kingdom **(I John 4:4)**.

Rom. 8:11
The Holy Spirit raised Jesus from the dead.
This same Holy Spirit indwells us and will one day raise us from the dead.

Matt. 4:1
Jesus submitted to the leading of the Holy Spirit. (God does not submit to anything below Himself.)

We should accept such leadership even if it goes against our comfort (wilderness) and ease (to be tempted-tested).

Acts 13:2-4

The Holy Spirit not only calls men to the ministry, but also calls them from one ministry to another (Antioch – prophets and teachers; to Cypress etc. – apostles).
The Holy Ghost is the sending agent for true gospel workers.

Acts 20:28

The Holy Ghost is to set the officers over the church.
Elections should be the members showing their understanding of how the Holy Spirit is working.

I Cor. 12:11

The Holy Spirit gives gifts to believers.
This is according to His own will, but that then is nothing other than the will of God – He is God!

HIS MINISTRY(S)

Gen. 1:2

He was and is active in <u>creation</u> (previously covered).
He <u>moves</u> before light breaks through.

Gen. 6:3

He <u>strives</u> with men.
There is a limit, and He is not to be taken for granted.

John 16:7-11

He <u>reproves</u> or convicts the world.
This is in three areas for three reasons.

II Thess. 2:5-7

He <u>restrains</u> (holds back) by being in the way of the normal flow of actions. He so controls that He determines what He will <u>let</u> and not let happen!
The wicked plots of men and the plans of the devil are all restricted to what the Holy Spirit allows (letteth) until He is taken out of the way.

John 3:3-8

He <u>births us</u> into the family of God.

CHAPTER 5: GOD THE HOLY SPIRIT

This opens up entrance into the Kingdom of God.

Rom. 8:9

He <u>indwells</u> the saved (**I Cor. 6:19, 20**).
Lack of this mark is evidence of being lost.

II Cor. 1:22

He <u>seals us</u> unto the day of redemption **(Eph. 1:13; 4:30)**.
He is the earnest of our inheritance – the down payment on what is to come!

Rom. 8:14

He <u>leads</u> us.
Calling (by separation, **Acts 13:2**); sending to location for service (**Acts 13:4**); and guidance in service (**Acts 3:27-29; 16:6-10**).

Rom. 8:16

He gives assurance of salvation.
This is definite, interior, and a witness to our spirit.
This task is Biblically reserved for the Holy Spirit and not to be attempted by humans.

Acts 1:8

He empowers the saints.
His working is needed for the Gospel to pierce through to the soul (**I Thess. 1:5**).
His working produces abundant hope in the saints (**Rom. 15:13**).

John 14:26

He teaches us (**I John 2:27**).
There are a variety of ways in which He teaches us:
He brings things to our remembrance. (**John 14:26**)
He reveals truths. (**I Cor. 2:10**)
He searches things out for us. (**I Cor. 2:10**)
He compares spiritual things with spiritual things. (**I Cor. 2:13**)
He testifies to us. (**John 15:26**)
He reproves. (**John 16:8**)
He guides. (**John 16:13**)
He speaks. (John 16:13; Rev. 2:7; I Tim. 4:1)
He shows us things to come. (**John 16:13**)
He glorifies Jesus. (**John 16:14**)

Eph. 3:16

The Holy Spirit strengthens us.
He has great might.
This work is in the inner man.

Rom. 8:2

He grants freedom from the law of sin and death.
There is a liberty given not by money, power, or government, but by the Holy Spirit – despite all obstacles (**II Cor. 3:17**).

Jude 20

He guides in prayer.
Various areas of prayer are under His guidance (**Eph. 6:18: Rom. 8:26, 27**).

Phil. 3:3

He guides us in worship.
He ministers to our spirit that our worship might be "*in spirit*" (**John 4:24**). Soul worship and physical (body) worship is unacceptable. Ritual, emotional, mental, and sensual stimuli cannot direct our worship. We need God the Holy Spirit to guide us.

John 16:14

He glorifies Jesus.
He doesn't speak of Himself but makes Jesus the issue.

Gal. 5:22, 23

He produces fruit in the lives of believers.
The fruit is singular – LOVE – all the rest is evidence of Biblical Love. Such fruit can only be produced by God working in us.

Rom. 8:11, 23

He has part in our future resurrection.
Our body is His temple and we are sealed unto the day of redemption – resurrection is guaranteed!

Rom. 8:1-27

He gives us victory over the flesh.
Verses 1-27 deal with a variety of aspects of how to obtain this victory.

Rom. 10:17

He helps produce faith.
It is not hearing the Bible that produces faith. Often that only produces intellectualism. It is hearing the Spirit <u>by</u> the Word of God that produces faith. His speaking through the Word helps us believe for salvation and proper Christian living.

I Cor. 6:11

He is involved in our sanctification.
Our cleansing, separation, dedication, and progressive holiness is tied to the inner working of the Holy Ghost who indwells us.

I John 2:27, 20

He provides knowledge.
Through Him there is nothing we <u>cannot</u> learn – we have a gift of information. We must learn how to access this knowledge.

Mark 13:11

He speaks through people.
He (in time of need) can and will tell us (or others) what to say.

II Cor. 13:14

The Holy Ghost communes with men.
He is not distant nor abstract. There is a real fellowship to be had.

BAPTISM(S)

There is no mention in the Bible of either a "baptism in the Spirit" or a "baptism of the Spirit." These are unbiblical terms and usually result in unbiblical practices and doctrines.

Baptism by the Spirit

I Cor. 12:12, 13 -

This is an action by the Holy Spirit.
The baptism is into the body of Jesus.
This is the means by which He places us into the proper place for service as He has gifted us.

Baptism with the Holy Ghost

John 1:32-24 -

This is an action by Jesus.
Acts 1:5, 6 – This is promised by Jesus.
Acts 11:15-18 – This is a clear sign of salvation.
Rom. 8:9 – The reception of the Holy Spirit is a mark of salvation.
This is a one-time action; never commanded; promised that we will receive; done by Christ; and a sign of salvation.
Some people confuse this with the filling of the Holy Spirit. Many older saints used the terms interchangeably. This has allowed for some of the Charismatic confusion of today. Terminology problems of one generation often lead to practical and doctrinal problems with later generations.

FILLING(S)

Eph. 5:18

This is a command.
Written to saved people (**Eph. 1:1**).
Burden of being filled falls on the individual.
Saved people are to receive this filling.
This is God's will (**Eph. 5:17**).

Eph. 5:19-6:18

Evidence of filling is clear, observable, and progressive.
It starts in the personal devotional life (**5:19, 20**).
It continues by showing in a submissive life in the Church (**5:21**).
Next it shows up in the home between husband and wife (**5:22-23**), children to parents (**6:1-3**), and fathers to children (**6:4**).
Lines of authority and responses show up as ways of evidencing the filling of the Holy Spirit. This is employee to boss (servants to masters **6:5-8** – bond or free) and boss to employee (**6:9**).
Only now is one ready to handle the spiritual warfare and our power/victory is based on obedience to being filled (**6:10-17**).
A useful prayer life is the climax and great evidence of filling (**6:18, 19**). This is far more than having occasional prayers answered.

Acts 2:1-12

The saints were filled at the day of Pentecost (**vs. 4**).
The use of the word "and" eight times in the first five verses shows that each item is separate and distinct.
Example: We don't have to have all believers in Jerusalem in full accord on the day of Pentecost for us to be filled today.

CHAPTER 5: GOD THE HOLY SPIRIT

Acts 4:8, 13
Peter was filled with the Holy Ghost.
This would be a second (or more) and subsequent filling to that of Pentecost.
It evidenced itself in a boldness and Christ likeness.

Acts 4:29-31
The church as filled here.
Peter was a part of the group and therefore filled a third time.
Filling is <u>not</u> a once-and-for-life event. It should be common and progressive.
It is possible for groups as well as individuals to be filled.

Acts 6:1-7
The filling of the Holy Ghost was a minimum qualification or a position of serving and responsibility in the Church.
These officers were caring for the feeding of the widows and thus relieving the others to care for the ministry of prayer and the Word.

Acts 7:54-60
Stephen was "**full of the Holy Ghost**" to the end of his life.
This made for a most honorable death.

Acts 9:17
Saul was already saved – called a brother.
He was now to be filled with the Holy Ghost.

Acts 11:22-24
Barnabas was full of the Holy Ghost.
This was requirement for ministering.

Acts 13:6-12
Saul/Paul was filled again with the Holy Ghost.
Filling is needed for people to see (not just hear) our doctrine.

Acts 13:50-52
Disciples filled with the Holy Ghost.
Joy goes with the filling.

Luke 4:1-2
Jesus was filled with the Holy Ghost.
Jesus was God in the flesh – how can we get along without filling?
Obviously not a removal of sin as Jesus had no sin.

Luke 1:15
John the Baptist was filled with the Holy Ghost from before birth.
This destroys many of men's theories regarding filling.
Filling is a supernatural act of God upon a mortal human.

Eph. 5:18
Filling is commanded.
Filling is compared to drinking:
keep drinking to be (or stay) filled.
affects thoughts, desires, speech, values, emotions, responses.

John 7:37-39
Drink to be filled.
In as a drink, out as a river – principle of expanded effect on others.
Overflow is for others – we stay filled.
Principle of Broken Vessel is to permit outflow.

Col. 3:15-16
God's peace and rulership.
Scriptures must dwell in us.
Total obedience and surrender are expected (compare **Eph. 5:19, 20**).

Gal. 5:16-24
Involves dealing with the flesh nature (the enemy of the Spirit.
Results in the fruit of the Spirit.

Eph. 4:22-24
Requires the putting off the "**old man**" – what we were.
Requires putting on "**the new man**" – what God designs us to become.

Luke 11:13
Filling is ours for the asking.
We are already indwelt as believers (**Rom. 8:9**).

Mark 11:24
We are to ask in faith.
We should examine to see if there is sin within which hinders our faith (and filling).

Three important questions:
Can I know I am filled?
Do you believe God's Word and what He has said?
Will you listen to the Holy Spirit bearing witness with our spirit?
Will you obey what is required?

Must I tarry, strive, etc.?
It's a gift, not earned.
No one ever tarried after Pentecost.
No Gentile ever tarried.

What are the manifestations?
Filling will release the Holy Spirit to work in and through you.
He reveals His nature, His fruits, His gifts, etc.
Results in godly Christian living with service.

HIS LEADING
To be governed, directed from within.

Jer. 10:23
Man cannot lead himself properly.
Man needs help.

Isa. 63:10-14
Moses did not lead on his own.
He let God lead him on how to lead others.
God's leading was that God's name might be honored.

Eph. 2:1-3
– Lost are led – by three, including the "***Spirit that now worketh***."

ILLUSTRATIONS:

Phillip and the Eunuch
Acts 8:27-29

Peter and Cornelius
Acts 10:19-20

Paul and Barnabas

Acts 13:2-4

Forbidden to preach in Asia

Acts 16:6, 7

PRINCIPLES:

Rom. 8:1-5
> Walk after the Spirit.
> Mind the things of the Spirit.

Rom. 8:13, 14
> Die daily.
> Led by the Spirit.
> Never leads contrary to the Scripture.
> Never leads contrary to the truth.
> In harmony with Scripture example and/or teaching.
> Always away from self (will, pleasing, confidence, image, discipline).
> Always toward God, His Power, Word, Kingdom, Program, Glory.
> Leads to a more holy life, separation from sin.
> Leads to Jesus (blood for guilt, love for forsaken, comfort for afflicted, etc.)

I John 4:1-4
> Holy Spirit wants us to check out Him versus other spirits as well as false speakers.

I Tim. 4:1
> There are demonic counterfeits.

II Thess. 2:1, 2
> We are not to be deceived.

Acts 16:16-18
> Satan may try to join our side to redirect, disrupt, or discredit.

Gal. 5:8
> Persuasion is not always of God.

Gal. 5:16-18
> Spirit and flesh are always at war.

HIS PART IN OUR FAITH AND PRAYER

CHAPTER 5: GOD THE HOLY SPIRIT

Heb. 11:1-3
Faith defined.
Faith is substance and evidence.

Heb. 11:6
Faith – believe God is.
Faith – believe God rewards.

Heb. 11:32-38
Things are accomplished by faith.

I Cor. 2:11-14
Things of God known and revealed by the Holy Spirit.
This includes the things freely given us.
Natural man knows nothing of these.

Rom. 8:6-8
Carnal mind is an enmity with God.

Rom. 8:22-26
Faith is related to hope (**Heb. 11:1-3**).
Holy Spirit has part in hope – therefore in faith.

Rom. 10:17
Faith cometh – doesn't dwell in us naturally.
Cometh by hearing – the Holy Spirit.
Hearing is by the Word of God.

SCRIPTURES:
Holy Spirit inspired
Holy Spirit taught
Holy Spirit applied
Holy Spirit speaking
Holy Spirit produces faith

Eph. 6:17
Word is the Sword of the Spirit.

Rom. 8:26, 27
Spirit helps in prayer.
Spirit makes intercession for us.

Zech. 12:10

Spirit involved in supplications.

Eph. 2:18
>Access in prayer to the Father is through the Spirit.

Eph. 6:18
>Prayer is to be in the Spirit (**Jude 20**).

Rom. 8:15
>Holy Spirit guides us in praying to the Father in a personal relationship "**Abba, Father**."

SINS AGAINST THE HOLY SPIRIT

Gen. 6:3
>Strive against Him.
>Resist His striving.

Isa. 63:9, 10
>Rebelled against Him.

Mark 3:29, 30
>Blaspheme against Him.

Acts 5:1-10
>Lie to Him (**vs. 3**).
>Tempt Him (**vs. 9**).

Acts 7:51
>Resist Him.

Eph. 4:30-32
>Grieve Him.

I Thess. 5:19
>Quench Him.

Heb. 10:26-31
>Despise – done despite to Him (**vs. 29**).

CHAPTER 6
MAN AND SIN
OUR CREATION

I Cor. 2:14
Lost are not likely to understand much about man's beginnings
Saved can and should know

Heb. 11:3
Creation can only be understood by faith (not by science, reason, study, etc.)
Creation was witnessed by no one but God
God has given us an account. Will we believe it?

Rev. 4:11
Creation is both a past and present activity.
All creation is for the pleasure of the Lord!

Heb. 2:6-8
Mankind was made/created
Mankind was crowned with glory and honor
Mankind set over all else in creation

Gen. 1:1, 2
Original Creation
Chaos appears – result of judgment

Gen. 1:26-28
Man made in God's image
Man in dominion over the rest of creation
Mankind made male and female
God's blessing given
be fruitful
multiply
replenish
subdue
have dominion

Gen. 1:29-30
    Man originally a vegetarian
    Animals were vegetarians

Gen. 2:7-9
    Man formed by God
    God gave us life
    God made us a soul
    God planted the Garden of Eden
    God placed man where He wanted him

Gen. 2:15-17
    God put man to work
    Man originally without sin
    Man warned – put on probation with a chance to exercise his will

Gen. 2:18-20
    Man needed a helpmeet
    Man showed great intellect in naming all the animals in less than a day
    Man's superiority shown in that no animal was qualified to be a helpmeet

Gen. 2:21-14
    Eve made from a rib of Adam
    Picture of marriage – from the beginning

Eccl. 7:29
    Man made perfect but chose sin

Eccl. 12:7
    Dust and spirit separate at death and go in different directions

Matt. 10:28
    Body and soul are different

Matt. 25:46
    Part of man is everlasting
    This is true for both the saved and the lost

I Thess. 5:23
    Man is a three part being
    Each area is capable of sin and is to be kept blameless

CHAPTER 6: MAN AND SIN

Our Fall
It is unknown how long man remained in a perfect condition before he fell into sin

Rom. 5:12-21
One Man (Adam) brought sin into the world
One man thus made us all sinners and brought death on the human race
We sin because we are sinners not sinners because we sin
it is our inherited nature
Problem of sin is inside us and works its way out into sinful actions
Since one man made all sinners, one man can thus save all.
 (Answer to: How can Jesus save more than one?)

Gen. 3:1
Satan appears as/or in a serpent.
Satan had already sinned
(Isa. 14:9-17, Ezek. 28:11-19).
He now moves to draw mankind into sin with him.
He chose the woman as his target.
the warning had been given to her husband
she should have remained under her husband's authority and protection
She listens to a creature which was supposed to be in subjection to her
likely near the forbidden tree
Satan casts doubt on God's Word, "**Hath God said?**"
Satan questions God's justice, love
magnified the "don't"
minimized the "do"
Satan's concept of freedom

Gen. 3:2, 3
Woman holds conversation with the enemy of herself, her husband, and God
She discusses the principles of God's Word to the neglect of the precise literal statements.
She tampers with God's Word
left out – "every" and "freely"
added – neither shalt thou touch it
softened – the issue of death

Gen. 3:4, 5
Satan denies that God will punish sin
Satan accuses God of selfishness, jealousy
Satan offers opportunity to become like the god<u>s</u> (demons)
Satan appeals to pride
Eve's compromise on the Scripture opens the door to greater attacks by Satan

Gen. 3:6-11

Eve chose to believe Satan and thus disbelieved God
I John 2:16
lust of the flesh – good for food
lust of the eyes – pleasant to the eyes
pride of life – desired to make one wise

She was deceived and ate
I Tim. 2:14
gave to her husband (no longer temptation)
Adam sins

Death comes <u>nine</u> ways
<u>Spiritual</u> – **Eph. 2:1** – immediate separation from God and His fellowship **Gen. 3:8**.
<u>Physical</u> – began immediately through depraved natures

Gen. 3:7, 10, 11; Titus 1:15

<u>Second Death</u> – final eternal separation from God in torment

Rev. 20:14, 15

<u>Economic</u> – separated from garden, easy living, and forced to labor hard
Gen. 3:17-19, 23, 24
<u>Equality</u> – man to rule over the woman and she to suffer in childbirth
Gen. 3:16; 1 Tim. 2:15
<u>Mental</u> – man's mind began to deteriorate with age and generationally
learning ability is still decreasing
<u>Moral</u> – showed in son Cain as a murderer
showed in son Cain as he argued with God

shame at nakedness
sodomy etc., gradually came ... a decreasing moral level generationally
Environmental – put out of the garden and never permitted to return exiled
Conscience – no repentance return
shift of blame
hid from God etc...

Sin Nature

Psm. 51:4

Sin is an act against a Holy God

Luke 15:18

Sin may also be against other people

Gal. 5:16-21

Sin is the result of the flesh nature at work
The Holy Spirit would fight against the flesh
Sin involves specific acts called *"works of the flesh"* – just acting according to our unchanged nature we were born with

Rom. 7:14

Paul is God's Biblical example of carnality
Adam (head of the race) sold us out to sin
By nature sin rules over us

DEFINITION OF SIN (14 DIFFERENT BIBLICAL ONES)

James 4:17   (1)

Knowing what to do and that it is good places a requirement on us. Not doing good is sin.

Jer. 14:7   (2)

Backsliding is sin
Any gap between us and God
We are to maintain close fellowship

Prov. 14:21   (3)

Despising your neighbor is sin
We are commanded to love our neighbors

Prov. 21:4 (4)
Pride is sin
We are commanded to be humble

Prov. 24:9 (5)
The thought of foolishness is sin
We are to be sober minded

Num. 21:7 (6)
Speaking against the Lord or His servant (leader of the people) is sin
We are to submit ourselves to God and His authority
God can easily deal with His servants

I Sam 15:23 (7 & 8)
Rebellion is sin – as is witchcraft
Similar in heart nature
Stubbornness is sin – as is iniquity and idolatry
We are to worship God only and without physical aids

Jer. 3:25 (9)
Not obeying the Lord is sin
God as creator has the right to expect our obedience

John 16:8, 9 (10)
Not believing on Jesus is sin
Repentance, Faith, being Born Again are requirements of God
He demands that we rest in faith on Jesus

Rom. 14:23 (11)
Anything not of faith is sin
God ordained that we should live by faith

I John 3:4 (12)
Transgression of the law is sin
God's law is to be obeyed

Jas. 2:9 (13)
Favoritism is sin
We are not to have respect of persons

I John 5:17 (14)
All unrighteousness is sin

We are expected to live righteously
I Cor. 6:9-10 – various gross forms of sin of the lost
Gal. 5:19-21 – various works of the flesh (sin)
Eph 4:30, 31 – various ways of sinning (grieving) against the Holy Spirit
Rev. 21:8 – various sins of those who will be lost for all eternity

PROGRESSION OF SIN

Rom. 1:18

God's wrath is against all sin
Men hold whatever truth they have in unrighteousness

Rom. 1:19-23

God has revealed truth
Man chooses to not give God glory
Men weren't thankful
Men's imagination and hearts affected
God's glory turned to religious imagery

Rom. 1:24-25

God then gives them up to uncleanness
Man goes into sin deeper

Rom. 1:26-27

God gives them up to vileness
Men move on to sexual perversion, sodomy, lesbianism, etc.

Rom. 1:28-32

God gives them over to a reprobate mind
Man goes into all types of sin, even sins worthy of death
They sin and enjoy those who are also as sinful as they are

RESULT OF SIN

Rom. 8:22

Creation groans in pain

GOD – CREATOR

Angels
Mankind
Animal Kingdom
Plant Kingdom

Mineral Kingdom

MAN WAS CREATED A LITTLE LOWER THAN THE ANGELS

Heb. 2:6, 7

Jude 6 – angels (sinning) already judged
Eccles. 7:20 – polluted the whole human race
Rom. 3:10, 19, 23 – all are guilty before God – depraved – rebels
Gen. 9:1-3 – Animal Kingdom suffered
 & e) **Gen. 3:17, 18** – Vegetable and Mineral (ground) Kingdoms suffered

Rom. 8:22

Man's sin affected all generations that followed, the whole race
Man's sin affected all of the rest of creation (except for the Angelic)

CHAPTER 7
WHAT IS SALVATION?

ABSOLUTE NEED TO BE SAVED

Salvation is not presented as an option, but as a requirement. Anything less displeases God and is SIN.

Heb. 11:5, 6

Enoch 'PLEASED GOD." This is the duty of man and a purpose for which we were created.
It takes faith to please God. Nothing less will satisfy Him.
There are two requirements for coming to God in faith:
belief in His existence and character
belief in His actions of rewarding those who seek Him
Belief must be genuine.
Seeking must be diligent, sincere, and continuous.
The issue is pleasing God, not pleasing man.

Acts 4:12

"We must be <u>SAVED</u>."
This is not a suggestion, but a necessity.

John 3:7

"Ye must be BORN AGAIN."
Another term to describe salvation, yet still a requirement.
Absolutely needed to see the Kingdom of God (John 3:3).
Must have it to enter the Kingdom of God (John 3:5).

Gal. 6:15

Only becoming "a NEW CREATURE" avails anything.
All of religion, religious acts, and religious ties are of no value apart from this change.

Eph. 2:1

We need to be "QUICKENED" or made alive.
Without this we are still dead in our sins – lost and in need of salvation.
Have you been saved, born again, quickened, made a new creature?
Do you please God?

I Cor. 2:14
> We need to be spiritual, – changed to something beyond a "natural man."
> We need God's change so that we can receive the things of the "Spirit of God" through discernment.
> This is a result of salvation, not education, intellect, or culture.

Jer. 13:23
> Only a supernatural change can produce a sufficient change of behavior.
> Self change is never adequate.

Jer. 17:9, 10
> Our hearts are corrupt by nature.
> Only God fully knows our heart.
> HE will reward us according to HIS analysis of our heart.

Luke 13:3, 5
> Perishing is the alternative to repenting.
> Jesus held to the necessity of repentance.

Luke 24:47, 48
> All nations are to hear the message preached by us.
> This message is two-fold:
> Repentance of sins
> Remission of sins
> There is a need for the sinner to have his sins removed from him.

Matt. 3:1, 2
> John the Baptist preached repentance.
> The availability of the Kingdom of Heaven requires repentance.
> Jesus preached the identical message in **Matt. 4:17**.

Mark 6:12
> Jesus sent the 12 out to preach repentance.
> message was an obligation, not an option.

Acts 26:20
> Paul preached the necessity of repentance.
> This message was given to both Jews and Gentiles.
> Turning to God follows repentance (turning from sin).

There are specific works that evidence true repentance (**II Cor. 7:11**).

John 3:16-18

To not believe is to be condemned already.
Jesus came to save us from our condemned condition.

John 3:36

Belief brings life, while unbelief brings wrath.
The sinner who doesn't act is condemned and under wrath for his inaction – unbelief.
The lost finds himself resisting the holy demands of Jesus to be saved, and ends up not believing Jesus – doubting Him, denying Him, etc.

THINGS WE ARE SAVED FROM

Matt. 16:24

We are saved from self, (ego) and its control of our lives.
Denial of self is similar to repentance.
We are delivered from self-centeredness, self-love, self-image, self-control, . . . SELF.

Matt. 18:11

We are saved from being LOST.
We were lost from God's usefulness, with a lost life, facing a lost eternity.
We were without right understanding of our location and condition, without proper direction, not knowing where we came from nor where we were going.

Mark 8:35

We are saved from a wasted life.
Most spend their lives trying to hold onto life, only to lose it in the end.
We can surrender our life for Jesus and the Gospel, and then enjoy it for these purposes.

Luke 4:18

We are saved from Satan and his demons.
Isa. 14:17 – "...opened not the house of his prisoners"
John 8:44 – Satan is father of all the lost.
Eph. 2:2, 3 – Spirits control the lost.

I John 3:8 – Works of the devil are destroyed.

Luke 7:48-50

We are saved from sin
Matt. 1:21 – gives the reason He was named "**Jesus**."
I John 3:9 – We no longer live in sin.
Rom. 6:17, 18, 22 – We are freed from sin.

John 3:15-18

We are saved from condemnation.
The lost are already condemned.

Acts 2:40

We are saved from this wicked generation.
"***Untoward***" means without direction, not toward a real or proper goal; perverse; stubborn; without reason.
They are untoward (not headed toward) holiness, virtue, heaven, worship of God, obedience to the Scriptures, enjoying God's promises and blessings.

Rom. 5:8, 9

We are saved from God's wrath.
This is accomplished by Jesus' blood.

II Thess. 2:9-12

We are saved from error.
They rejected the love of the truth.
Salvation brings us to the truth (**I Tim. 2:4**).

Heb. 2:15

We are saved from the fear of death.
The lost have much to fear.
We have no need to fear going to Jesus.

Heb. 4:9-11

We are saved from our own efforts.
They are traps, burdens, blocks from coming to God.
By faith we can enter into true rest.

SALVATION IS ETERNAL

The believer is secure; preservation is shown by perseverance.

CHAPTER 7: WHAT IS SALVATION?

John 3:15, 16, 36

Our salvation involves receiving Life from God.
This Life is eternal, having neither beginning nor end.
This Life is everlasting, never ending.
This Life by definition is God's Life and permanent.

John 4:14

Christ's water leaves a permanent change, - **"never thirst."**
The **"never"** thirsting again is emphasized by the **"everlasting"** benefit of life.

John 5:24

The **"everlasting life"** is not a future to be gained, but the present to be experienced – **"hath."**
A result of **"everlasting life"** is that we will never come into condemnation.
Another result is that we have **"passed"** (by resurrection power) **"from death unto life."**

John 6:27

"Everlasting Life' should be our goal and gift received.
We are to avoid what doesn't last – **"meat that perisheth."**

John 6:39, 40, 47, 54

"Everlasting Life" involves being given by the Father to Jesus.
The Father has willed that Jesus **lose none** of those with everlasting life.
Jesus has promised to lose none and **"will raise"** us up at the last day.

John 6:68, 69

Peter understood about **"eternal life."**
Peter knew that Jesus was the source of life without beginning or ending.

John 10:27, 28

Jesus taught that **His sheep** had **eternal life** and would **never perish**.
He made it clear that no act of any man could remove one soul out of His grip or His Father's.

John 11:25, 26

When we believe we receive life and "***shall never die***" (spiritually). Jesus wants us to believe this.

John 17:1-3

This "***eternal life***" is not only a truth and a doctrine, it is a reality that involves KNOWING the Father and the Son.
Only those given to Jesus receive this life and knowledge of God in a personal sense.

John 20:31

The purpose of the Gospel of John was to lead people to LIFE.
Other books tell more on this lasting relationship as well as about other issues.

BY GRACE ALONE, THROUGH FAITH ALONE

Heb. 11:6

God will not be pleased without our exercising faith.
We must believe in His existence, person, nature, and actions.
True faith will seek God diligently until rewarded.

Titus 2:11

God's salvation is brought to mankind by God's grace.
No grace, no salvation.

Eph. 2:4-10

Grace is the means by which we are saved, not works.
Faith is our response, and is evidenced by God's changing us to walk in good works.

John 1:12, 13

Because of God's grace, through faith we can receive Jesus as He is, – not as we imagine Him to be.
This birth is not due to our family, our will or anyone else's will. It is of God.

Rom. 1:16

By faith we lay hold of the Gospel of Christ.
The Gospel is the power of God, – not our works or worth.

Rom. 10:9-17

True faith is a heart issue and evidences itself with righteous living.

True faith never leaves us ashamed.
True faith results in a real salvation.
True faith comes by hearing God speak to us by the Word of God.

Gal. 3:22-29

True faith is not ours, – we are not born with it.
True faith is actually the "**faith of Jesus Christ**" (**vs. 22**).
True faith comes to us (**vss. 23, 25**).
True faith is revealed **_after_** the law has been applied (**vs. 23**).
True faith is the basis of our being justified and our becoming the children of God (**vss. 24, 26**).

Heb. 4:9-11

True faith involves ceasing from our own works.
True faith is to be sought with all energy possible.

I John 5:4

True faith gives us victory in overcoming the world.
This product of faith is evidence of being born of God.

I John 5:11-13

True faith leads to a know-so salvation.
True faith is a result of God's written Word.

James 2:14-26

True faith produce works.
No works and faith is dead.

Rom. 12:3

Grace is a gift to us.
This grace is a means by which we are to speak.

Heb. 12:2

Jesus is the source and designer (author) of our faith.
Jesus also produces, provides, and completes (finishes) our faith.

A FULL (COMPLETE) SALVATION

I Thess. 5:23

God looks at the "**whole**" of the three-part man – "**spirit, soul, and body**."
"**Preserved blameless**" implies a full salvation that brought them to a blameless condition. Now the issue is to stay blameless.

I Thess. 5:5

Salvation brings a complete change; night to day and darkness to light.
There is no grey area of mixture.

I Thess. 4:7

Salvation brings a clear call from God to holiness.
We have been delivered from uncleanness.

II Cor. 5:17

Being saved puts us in Christ.
We become new creatures, old things are passed away, <u>all</u> things become new.

II Cor. 7:10, 11

Salvation must be preceded by a God-produced sorrow and working repentance.
There are <u>seven</u> clear signs or fruits of repentance:
CAREFULNESS – careful to never again fall into this sin, – careful to avoid what leads to this sin.
CLEARING – confession, restitution, clearing of damage.
INDIGNATION – greatly stirred over ever falling into this sin(s) and indignant against sin.
FEAR – a fear of God and a fear of falling back into the sin. We know the weakness of our flesh.
VEHEMENT DESIRE – a great desire to do right and a loving and great desire towards Jesus.
ZEAL – zealous for the Kingdom, souls of men, righteousness, etc.
REVENGE – against the sins we have committed with a desire to rescue others from it and attack the sin itself.
Real salvation will bring great changes on the sin issue.

II Cor. 5:20

We have become Christ's ambassadors to a lost and rebellious world.
The need is for God's enemies to be reconciled by Jesus.

Rev. 1:5, 6

Our sins are washed from us in Jesus' blood.
We are made kings and priests unto God – both horizontal and vertical ministries.

Acts 26:18
>Our eyes are opened spiritually.
>We are turned from darkness to light.
>We are turned from the power of Satan unto God.
>We have received forgiveness of sins and an inheritance among other saved.

Matt. 16:24
>We have denied self for Jesus' sake.
>We have taken up our cross to follow Jesus.

John 14:16, 17
>The Holy Ghost (**vs. 26**) is given to us as a Comforter.
>The world cannot receive Him but He is with us "***foreve**r.*"
>He also ministers to us as the "***Spirit of Truth.***"
>We are indwelt by deity, – the entire trinity.
>**vs. 17** – The Holy Ghost in us.
>**vs. 20** – Jesus in us.
>**vs. 23** – The Father in us.

Rom. 8:9
>Not only is the Holy Spirit in us, but we are in Him.
>Those without the Spirit of Christ are still lost.

Rom. 8:14
>We are given divine leadership by the Spirit of God.
>There is a difference between His leading and our following.

Rom. 8:16
>There is a divine witness within by the Holy Spirit.
>This witness is to our spirit.

Rom. 8:35-39
>We humbly live as sheep accounted for the slaughter.
>We are more than conquerors through Jesus.
>Nothing shall separate us from God's love as found in Jesus our Lord.

Titus 2:11-14
>God's grace teaches us.
>We are taught to:
>deny ungodliness

deny worldly lusts
live soberly
live righteously
live godly
look for Jesus' return.
We are redeemed from **all** iniquity.
Jesus purifies us for Himself
to be a peculiar people
to be zealous of good works.

Rom. 6:23

We are delivered from eternal death.
We are given eternal life.

Eph. 2:1

We are quickened or made alive (**vs. 5**) in salvation through Jesus.
We "*were*" (in the past now) in trespasses and sins, but are now delivered.

John 3:16

We now enjoy everlasting life.
We have entered into a life of believing and will have no fear of perishing.

I Pet. 1:3-5

We have a lively hope.
We have an inheritance:
incorruptible
undefiled
that never fades away and
is reserved in Heaven.
We are kept by the power of God.

I John 1:3

We can now fellowship with other Christians.
We have fellowship with both God the Father and with Jesus Christ.

I John 1:7, 9

We have both cleansing and forgiveness of our sins.
This acts in "**all**" our sins.

I John 2:3

We can know for sure that we KNOW God.

CHAPTER 7: WHAT IS SALVATION?

This is evidenced by keeping God's commandments.

I John 3:14
We by spiritual nature love the brethren.
A lack of love is evidence of being lost.

I John 5:4
We do overcome the world.
This victory is through our faith.

Heb. 10:38, 39
We live by faith.
We shall continue following and not draw back.

SALVATION IS THROUGH JESUS AND HIS WORK ALONE

John 14:6
Jesus is:
the way to God,
the truth about God, and
the life of God.
Only by Jesus can anyone come to the Father.

Acts 4:12
Salvation is in no one else.
Jesus is the only name that will produce salvation among men.

John 1:12
Only by receiving Jesus might the sinner be saved.
Belief in Jesus' name is a requirement.

John 1:29
Jesus is God's Lamb for sinners.
He alone takes away our sin.

John 3:14-21
Jesus, the Son of Man, was lifted up for us to believe in Him (**vss. 14, 15**).
Jesus, the Son of God, was sent by the Father for us to believe in (**vs. 16**).
God sent Jesus that the world might be saved (**vs. 17**).
Belief in Jesus is the only way to escape condemnation (**vs. 18**).

Acts 16:31
> Only one way is given to be saved.
> Belief must be in the Lord Jesus Christ

Rom. 5:6-11
> "*Christ died for us*" (vss. 6, 7, 8, 10).
> We are "*justified by HIS blood*" (vss. 9, 11).
> We are "saved from wrath through HIM" (vs. 9).
> We are "reconciled by HIS death" (vs. 10).
> We are "*saved by HIS life*" (vs. 10).
> It is all "through our Lord Jesus Christ" (vs. 11).

Rom. 6:23
> God's gift is through Jesus Christ.
> Eternal life only comes through Jesus Christ.

Rom. 10:9, 10
> Confession is only of the Lord Jesus.
> Belief is only in Jesus' resurrection.

I Cor. 15:3, 4
> The Gospel is of Jesus.
> It is:
> Christ's death,
> Christ's burial, and
> Christ's resurrection

Gal. 3:26-29
> Becoming a child of God requires faith in Christ Jesus.
> It is Christ we put on; Christ we are baptized in.
> Our oneness is in Christ Jesus.
> Only as we are Christ's are we heirs to the promise.

Gal. 4:4, 5
> God's plan of salvation and timing are centered in Jesus.
> Our redemption and adoption are through Jesus.

Eph. 1:7
> Redemption is in Jesus; through HIS Blood.
> Our forgiveness of sins is according to the riches of HIS grace.

CHAPTER 7: WHAT IS SALVATION?

Eph. 2:10, 13
We are "created in Christ Jesus."
We are "***made nigh***" by the blood of Christ.

I John 5:11, 12
Our eternal life is in Jesus.
Without Jesus there is no eternal life. (A man may have a decision, baptism, doctrine, works, soul winning, prayers, church membership, etc., but without Jesus he is lost.

Rev. 5:8-10
Jesus has redeemed us by His blood.
Jesus made us kings and priests.

John 5:39
Men look for eternal life in the Scriptures.
The emphasis of the Scriptures is on revealing Jesus.
We need Jesus for eternal life as it cannot be had apart from HIM.

Luke 24:25-27, 44
All of the Scriptures speak of Jesus.
They tell of Christ's sufferings and the glory that should follow.

NATURE OF SAVING FAITH

Heb. 11:6
It takes faith to please God.
This faith was clearly defined.
Not just any kind of faith will do.
There are two kinds of faith:
Natural and
Supernatural (Saving)

John 2:23-25
These believed but Jesus did not commit Himself to them.
Only a faith that changes the inside ever satisfies Jesus.
Their faith was based on physical sight, –
"They saw."

John 12:42-43
These had a faith, but it wasn't enough to bring them to "***confess***" Jesus.

Their faith was smaller than their love of the praise of men.

Acts 8:13-23

Simon "***believed***" but was perishing (**vss. 20, 21**).
His faith was an act affected by bitterness (**vs. 23**), loss of a following (**vss. 9-13**), and a misunderstanding of God's gifts (**vs. 20**).

James 2:19, 20

Some have a faith that is dead.
Devils have a faith and it makes them tremble.
Such faith (**John 2 & 12: Acts 8; James 2**) is natural and insufficient.

John 1:12, 13

There is a faith that leads to becoming a son of God.
This faith is tied to being born of God.

Eph. 2:8-10

Supernatural faith is tied to God's grace.
This faith leaves us nothing about which to boast.

Gal. 1:23

True faith is to be preached.
It isn't natural, – it must be preached into men's hearts.

Gal. 2:16

Justification is based on faith.
The type of faith is not ours (natural), but Christ's faith (supernatural).

Gal. 2:20

Christ's faith is given to us to live by.
The source means that the quality and quantity are plenty.

Gal. 3:22, 24, 25

Christ's faith is given to us to be able to believe.
It gives us access to the promise.
Right faith frees us from the bondage of the law.

Rom. 10:17

The needed faith is not natural, but comes to us.
It comes from Christ (**Galatians**).

CHAPTER 7: WHAT IS SALVATION?

It comes by hearing . . . God speak.
This hearing comes by the Word of God.

Heb. 11:1-3

Supernatural faith is substance and evidence.
Through it we understand God's works.

Heb. 11:4-39

Faith produces action:
vs. 4 – a more excellent sacrifice
    5 – translation to Heaven
7 – built an ark
8 – left home at God's direction
9 – lived in the land of promise
11 – received strength to conceive
17 – offered up a son
20 – blessed a son
21 – blessed his sons and worshipped
22 – gave commands regarding burial
23 – were not afraid of the King's commandment
24 – refused high position, chose to suffer
27 – forsook Egypt
28 – kept the Passover
29 – passed through the Red Sea
30 – walls of Jericho fell down
31 – deliverance from Jericho
33 – subdued kingdoms, wrought righteousness, obtained promises, stopped the mouths of lions,
  34 – quenched the violence of fire, escaped the edge of the sword, out of weakness were made strong, waxed valiant in fight, ran enemies off
35 – women received dead raised to life, were tortured, etc.
39 – received a good report.

James 2:14, 17, 20, 26

Faith should be evidenced by works.
No works means the faith is dead (natural faith) and useless for salvation.
Faith that can produce proper works (supernatural faith) is profitable for salvation.

CHAPTER 8
WHAT IS THE CHURCH?

THE CHURCH
UNIVERSAL AND LOCAL

Two concepts are found in the Scriptures. The emphasis Biblically is heavily weighted towards the "local" concept. – The word "church" is often misused.

Eph. 1:22, 23

Jesus is the head of the Church.
Jesus is the head over "**all things**" to the Church – in <u>all</u> areas, functions, plans, goals, principles, methods, decisions, motives, etc.
The Church is Christ's body here on earth.
The Church is to fully do Christ's work on earth as instructed by Jesus, the Head.
This pictures the Church in its large view.

I Thess. 1:1

This refers to a specific group in a local area made up of specific people.
They were the receivers of this book.
Other such churches were addressed:

Rom. 1:7	Phil. 1:1
I Cor. 1:2	Col. 1:2
II Cor. 1:1	II Thess. 1:1
Eph. 1:1	

Saved people (saints) were gathered together to function as a unit called a church.

Gal. 1:2

This refers to more than one church – "**churches**" – thus specific groups throughout a region.
Rev. 1:4 – The book of Revelation was sent to seven different churches in seven different cities (**2:1, 8, 12, 18; 3:1, 7, 14**).
Each church was distinct from the others with specific traits, problems, etc.

Acts 15:13-18

God designed to visit the Gentiles and "**take out**" a people.
God knew all of His actions well ahead of time – "**from the beginning.**"

Acts 16:5

Churches are to be "established in the faith."
They are also to be "increased in number daily."
This was the result of being ministered to.

Matt. 16:13-18

This is the first mention of the word "***church***" in the Bible.
The Church belongs to Jesus – "***My Church***."
The Church is built by Jesus. Anything built by man cannot be a church.
The "***gates of Hell***" can never prevail against the Church.
Jesus will build His Church on "***this rock***."
Not Peter – he was only a stone.
Not verbal agreement to right doctrine (**7:22, 23**).
Involved divine revelation of the person of Christ (**vss. 16, 17 & 11:25-27**).

Matt. 18:15-17

The local church is a place for hearing of disputes, coming to conclusions, and passing judgments in discipline.
This even covers the area of faults and trespassing.

Eph. 5:22-33

Marriage is a picture of the relationship of Christ and His Church.
This passage deals primarily with Christ and the Church (**vs. 32**)!
Disruption of the marriage relationship mars the picture of the Church.
The wife is to picture the Church in …
Her submission (**vs. 22).**
Not being the head (**vs. 23**).
Being saved (**vs. 23**).
Her subjection (**vs. 24**).
Recipient of love (**vs. 25**).
Being sanctified and cleansed (**vs. 26**).
Being holy and without blemish (**vs. 27**).
Being joined permanently as one to her husband (**vs. 31**).
Reverencing her husband (**vs. 32**).

CHAPTER 8: WHAT IS THE CHURCH?

Eph. 3:3-11

The Church with Gentile members "***was not known***" (**vs. 5**) in previous ages.

Now the mystery of the Church is to be revealed not only to mankind (**vs. 5**), but also to principalities and powers (**vs. 10**).

The Church is to illustrate the great wisdom of God.

I Cor. 12:12, 13

We are baptized by the Holy Spirit into the Church.

We are individual members with individual ministries, yet one body joined together under Jesus.

I Cor. 12:27-31

God has chosen the area of function for each member, and the importance or priority of that function.

No one is able to fill all of the functions and no one function is held by all.

We need each other for the Church to function properly (**Rom. 12:4, 5**).

Col. 1:13-18

Jesus is to have the pre-eminence in the Church, – not man, men, leaders, committees, doctrine, building, tradition, program, etc.

Jesus is to be the focus, message, concern, delight, and the passion of the Church.

PURPOSE AND FUNCTION

Eph. 2:19-22

Not only are we individually indwelt by the Holy Spirit (**I Cor. 6:19, 20**), but we are to be jointly as a church inhabited by God through the Holy Spirit.

Jesus is the Chief Corner Stone of His Church.

We are built on the foundation of the apostles and prophets.

We are not randomly thrown together but "***fitly framed together***" by God.

We are to grow in holiness both individually and corporately into a temple in the Lord.

Eph. 3:7-10

The Church is the receiver of God's minister(s), and to benefit from their preaching.

The Church is to operate according to the eternal purpose of God as seen in Christ Jesus our Lord.

God's (many-sided) wisdom is put on display before an onlooking world of humanity and angelic beings. It is seen in the Biblically functioning Church!

Eph. 3:20, 21

The Church is to display the glory of God for all to see.

God answers Church prayer beyond what we ask or think that there might be glory in the Church.

This glory is produced by Jesus in the Church.

This glory should be constant through all ages and circumstances, and never end!

Eph. 4:7-16

(**vs. 11**). Jesus assigns ministers to churches as gifts. They are not deserved, earned, nor to be taken for granted.

Churches should not choose a minister but seek to find Christ's gift to them if and when a need arises. It would be a devastating event to lose, abuse, or send away Christ's gift and replace him with a non-given professional or amateur who wasn't God's choice.

Different ministers have different ministries and are not to be compared or contrasted with each other.

(**vs. 12**). The function of the minister is ...

To bring the saints into conformity to the Bible,

To develop the saints so that they can minister to a lost world,

To instruct and strengthen the Church.

It is <u>not</u> the duty of the minister to reach the world, but rather to work with the Church. The Church is to reach the world. (Shepherds work with sheep and sheep have lambs).

(**vs. 13**). The minister's work is to continue in the church <u>until</u> ...

The whole Church is in unity of "**the faith**."

The whole Church has a full knowledge of Jesus in all His aspects.

The whole Church is made up of holy people.

The whole Church measures up to being fully conformed into the image of Jesus.

(**vs. 14**) The minister labors in the Church and the people follow so that they might reach a place of doctrinal stability. They become so instructed that no one can manipulate, deceive, or pull them from the truth.

(**vs. 16**) The Church so develops that it ...

CHAPTER 8: WHAT IS THE CHURCH?

    Stays "***joined together***" in a fit way.
    Increases in members.
    Edifies itself in love.

I Cor. 12:28

God knows what each Church needs in ministry and who is to be placed where.
God sets people in the Church according to His wisdom.
He only gives a church "***some***", not all.

Acts 20:28

God's Church was purchased with His blood (blood of deity).
The "***elders of the Church***" (**vs. 17**) were to feed the flock.
The Holy Ghost had made these elders "overseers" <u>over</u> the Church.
The Church is never to be over the elders.

Acts 16:5

The churches were first to be established in the faith.
After establishing of the Church, then comes the increasing in number … possibly even on a daily basis.

Acts 2:41

Entrance into the local Church requires:
Hearing the word.
Gladly receiving the Word.
Scriptural baptism.
Uniting with the Church.
(**vs. 42**) This will be followed by:
Continuing steadfastly in right doctrine and fellowship.
Bonding and visiting with each other (**vss. 42, 44-46**).
Continuing steadfastly in a life of prayer.

Acts 2:47

The Church should constantly praise God.
The lives of its members should be above reproach and find favor with all.
Additions to the Church will be based on their faithfulness.

Eph. 5:21-23

The Church should have a fear of God.
The members of the Church must learn to submit to each other.

II Cor. 11:2

The Church is to be as a chaste virgin.

The Church is already espoused to Jesus.

Paul exercised a "**godly jealousy**" over the Church at Corinth to keep her pure. This pattern should be followed by all who love Jesus.

Impurity in the espousal relationship was reason for either a public stoning or a private being put away (**Matt. 1:19**).

Acts 12:5

The Church must recognize the great power of prayer.

In time of stress, the Church turned to prayer and succeeded. They bypassed the lesser matters of petitions, politics, lawyers, marches, protests, organizations, pub-lishing, complaining, etc.

(**Col. 4:2-4**) Prayer can open doors for speaking, helps us make the mystery of Christ known, and be able to speak as we should.

(**II Thess. 3:1**) Prayer gives the Word of God freedom to operate in hearts and be glorified in others as it is in us.

(**Rom.15:30,31**)Prayer can bring deliverance from unbelieving persecutors and accep-tance of service. Believers must put efforts into striving together in prayer.

(**II Cor. 1:11**) Prayer as a church is a means of helping God's servants when they are in desperate situations (**vss. 9 & 10**).

A church will only make progress as it makes it in prayer on their knees.

Eph. 6:18, 19

Prayer is the basis of the spiritual warfare (**10-17**).

Prayer is to be constant (always), in all areas, and with supplication "**in the Spirit**."

Prayer for all saints by the Church is to be normal.

Prayer makes possible right speaking, boldness, and the ability to make clearly known the mystery of the Gospel.

Phil. 1:9, 10

Prayer produces increased love, knowledge, and judgment.

Sincerity and being inoffensive come from right praying.

Phil. 1:19

Paul expected deliverance from suffering through the prayers of the Church.

CHAPTER 8: WHAT IS THE CHURCH?

Prayer can and should be mixed with the work of the Holy Spirit. The Church is the mixing place.

I Cor. 6:1-5

The Church is the place where believers can have their differences settled.

Saints will one day judge angels. Issues of human matters are far simpler and should be able to be handled easily in the Church.

Phil. 4:10-19

The Church is to corporately support missionaries in their labors.

The Church, and thus its members, receives credit for supported missionaries' fruit. It is recorded on their account.

The Church that sacrifices (**vs. 18**) for missionaries receives special promises:

(**vs. 13**) Strength to do all things.

 (**vs. 19**) Supplies to meet our needs.

Acts 13:1-5

The Church was the location from which the first missionaries were selected.

The Church was informed by the Holy Ghost whom they should send.

The missionaries had first proved their usefulness and had gained experience in the local Church.

The sending of the missionaries (including the commissioning) was accomplished by the Church.

Matt. 9:37, 38

Jesus taught that prayer affects the production and sending of laborers.

There is a difference between laborers and volunteers, novices, etc. Laborers are experienced, active, capable, productive, etc. The Church is the preparation place for laborers.

I Tim. 3:5

Pastors are to care for the Church of God as they rule their own houses.

Rebels against pastoral authority are like rebellious children in the home.

I Tim. 3:14, 15

The Church is God's house – not the building, but the people.

The Church is owned by and controlled by a God who is very much alive.

It is essential to know how to behave in the membership of the Church.

The Church is God's custodian/proclaimer of Truth to this sinful generation.

Heb. 2:11, 12

Jesus has a special relation with the people of His Church(es) – He calls us "**brethren**."

Jesus joins with the Church in its worship and sings with us to praise God the Father! This would have to be a local Church!

James 2:1-9

The Church is not to judge individuals based on their person, wealth, jewelry, clothing, etc.

The assembly is where all believers are equal before God. We are to set apart those distinctions and prejudices found out in the world.

CHURCH DISCIPLINE

This is corrective discipline, not formative discipline. Different problems are to be dealt with differently. There is no one way to deal with all different problems. There is a great variety of offences and ways of handling each.

Matt. 18:15-17

Trespass is a "fault", not a sin.

Faults are to be confessed to others (James 5:16), while sins are confessed to God (I John 1:9).

The trespass is a breaking over that is personally offensive and serious.

The 'fault" is to be approached on an individual basis by the offended party, OR the offender may approach the offended party and confess his fault asking for prayer (James 5:16). Consider (Rom. 15:1 and Gal. 6:1, 2).

If the offender refuses to face his fault, further steps are outlined to deal with their stubbornness (I John 1:8 and I Tim. 6:4).

Often, dealing with a fault uncovers deeper and more serious issues. The final step is to put them out of the Church and treat them as lost.

CHAPTER 8: WHAT IS THE CHURCH?

Acts 5:1-10

(vs. 3) The offense was a deliberate lie to the Holy Ghost.
The price was death (vss. 4, 5, and 10). This is somewhat similar to Achan in the O. T.
This is totally different than Matt. 18:15-17.
It is not a fault but a sin. It is not a trespass against Peter, but a lie to the Holy Ghost.
There is a sin unto death (I John 5:16-17).
(vss. 11-14) These verses give five results of this discipline.

Rom. 16:17, 18

The offence here is, "<u>cause divisions and offenses</u>." This goes beyond disagreements.
There is no particular doctrine at issue.
They are operating so as to break the unity of the Spirit and the bond of peace.
These serve their own belly.
These are good talkers – "**good words and fair speeches**", but they deceive the hearts of the simple.
We are to "<u>mark them</u>" and "<u>avoid them</u>."

I Cor. 5:1-13

The guilt is of <u>serious sin</u> (**vs. 11; 6:9-10**).
The guilty party is called a brother, but acts like the lost.
Action to take is: <u>Deliver to Satan</u> (**vs. 5**), Purge out (**vss. 7 and 13**) <u>Not to keep company</u> (**vs. 11**), <u>not to eat with</u> (**vs. 11**), and <u>Judge</u> (**vs. 12**).
Results may or may not be to recover the sinner. The primary goal is the purity and protection of the Church (**vs. 7**) and regaining sincerity and truth in the Church (**vs. 8**).

I Cor. 11:16

Issue of somebody who would <u>seem to be contentious.</u>
This is <u>not to be tolerated</u>. We have no such custom in the Church.

I Thess. 5:14

Some are <u>unruly,</u> i.e., they don't submit to being ruled.
Such we are to <u>warn</u>...
of dangers.
of sin against the Holy Spirit.
of reaping.
of damaging a testimony.

of lost opportunities.
of lack of Christ-likeness.

II Thess. 3:6-15

A group of offenses often related are here listed:
(**vs. 6**)   Walking disorderly
(**vs. 11**) <u>Lazy</u>
(**vs. 11**) Busy bodies.
The responses are just as clear:
(**vs. 6**)   Withdraw yourself from them
(**vs. 14**) Note that man
(**vs. 14**) Have no company with him.
Don't treat such as an enemy or lost, but rather as a brother.
Admonish, let them be ashamed, but don't reject totally.
Often this reveals the weakness within the Church as some individual members may not co-operate in breaking fellowship as commanded in the Bible. These may become guilty of **vs. 6**, – walking disorderly or being unruly (**I Thess. 5:14**).

I Tim. 1:19, 20

These had <u>blasphemed</u> – <u>bad doctrine</u> (**II Tim. 2:17, 18**).
They were to be <u>delivered unto Satan</u>. The purpose was to teach them a lesson not to shipwreck or overthrow the faith of others.

I Tim. 5:19, 20

This deals with the problem of <u>elders in sin</u>.
Accusations are to be given by a minimum of two witnesses.
The accusations are not to be received except "***before***" or in the presence of the accused elder.
If he is found guilty, there is to be a <u>public rebuke.</u>
Examples include Paul rebuking Peter (**Gal. 2:11**) and John rebuking Diotrophes (**III John 7-9**).

Titus 3:10, 11

Here is the case of an heretick.
Such is subverted, sinneth, and condemned of himself.
They are to receive <u>two admonitions</u>, and if they do not repent, then <u>reject them</u>.

CHAPTER 8: WHAT IS THE CHURCH?

OFFICERS OF THE CHURCH

Titus 1:5-11 (cf. I Tim. 3:1-7)

Elders are found in the plural in the cities and churches (**Acts 14:23; 20:17; Titus 1:5**).

Bishops are found in the singular (**Titus 1:7; I Tim. 3:1, 2**) with the exception of **Phil. 1:1.**

Bishops must meet all the requirements of the elders and seem to hold both titles simultaneously. (All bishops are elders, but not all elders are bishops).

Requirements include:
Blameless (**Titus 1:6**)
Husband of one wife (**vs. 6**)
Having faithful children **vs. 6**)
Not self-willed (**vs. 7**)
Not soon angry (**vs. 7**)
Not given to wine (**vs. 7**)
Not given to filthy lucre (**vs. 7**)
A lover of hospitality (**vs. 8**)
A lover of good men (**vs. 8**)
Sober (**vs. 8**)
Just (**vs. 8**)
Holy (**vs. 8**)
Temperate (**vs. 8**)
Well taught (**vs. 9**)
Holding fast to the faithful word (**vs. 9**)
Consistent to what he had been taught (**vs. 9**)
Able to exhort and convince gainsayers (**vs. 9**)
Able to stop mouths (**vs. 11**)
Vigilant (**I Tim. 3:2**)
Of good behavior (**vs. 2**)
Apt to teach (**vs. 2**)
No striker (**vs. 3**)
Patient (**vs. 3**)
Not a brawler (**vs. 3**)
Not covetous (**vs. 3**)
Ruling his own house (**vs. 4**)
Children under subjection (**vs. 4**)
Not a novice (**vs. 6**)
Good reputation in the world (**vs. 7**).

II Tim. 3:8-13

Deacons are found in the plural in the churches (**I Tim. 3:8; Phil. 1:1**).

While the bishop is the pastor, leader, shepherd, overseer, and the elders assist as overseers, the deacons seem to assist, support, strengthen the hands of the pastor. They certainly are not to rule over the shepherd.

Requirements include:
Grave (v**s. 8)**
Not double tongued (**vs. 8**)
Not given to much wine (**vs. 8**)
Not greedy of filthy lucre (**vs. 8**)
Hold the mystery of the faith (**vs. 9**)
Must be first tested and proved (**vs. 10**)
Blameless (**vs. 10**)
Wives must be grave (**vs. 11**)
Husband of one wife (**vs. 12**)
Ruling both children and house well (**vs. 12**)
Great benefits to faithful service (**vs. 13**).

The high requirements for these church officers allows the Church to set a model before new Christians and the world of how homes and lives should be. Thus every generation can come back to holy lives and holy homes by God's ordained means.

THE CHURCH AND THEIR PASTOR

I Thess. 5:12-14

Know them; that is, recognize God's servant as God's servant, spiritually accept his ministry, love him as God loves him, receive him as God's minister and messenger.

Esteem them; that is value him and his ministry, attend regularly, co-operate and encourage him, treat with the highest respect, and avoid criticism, bitterness, rumors, jealously, and familiarity.

Be at peace; an improper attitude brings dissension, lack of peace, and turmoil (warn the unruly).

Eph. 4:11-16

Pastors are a gift to the Church from Jesus. He is free to give them to another Church at anytime.

With a shortage of laborers (and an oversupply of self-approved, trained volunteers) it often happens that churches end up with

CHAPTER 8: WHAT IS THE CHURCH?

hirelings instead of God-given shepherds (pastors) (**John 10:12, 13**).
Don't resist or avoid the ministry of a God-given pastor.

Heb. 13:17, 7

Obey and submit to them (**I Tim. 3:4, 5**).
Let them care for your soul.
Your response to them may determine the destiny of your soul and/or others (presently, for future generations, visitors, society).

Psm. 105:15

Touch not mine anointed.
If He protected Israel, how much more His people today.
When God has His hand on a man, He never lets anyone else put their hands on him.

I Sam. 24:6, 10; 26:9, 11, 23

Daniel wouldn't touch wicked Saul, even in self defense.

II Sam. 1:14-16

Death was the proper punishment for claiming to destroy God's anointed.

I Cor. 9:7-14

Oxen get the first choice and their fill from the harvest.
Spiritual ministering brings material results.

I Tim. 5:17-20

Faithful ministers are worthy of double the income of their people.
Levites in the O. T. received a tithe (10%) from the other 12 tribes. The Levites were the smallest tribe, and thus had an income of over three times the average Israelite when all gave as they should (**Num. 1:45-47; 3:39**). This was before first fruit offerings, love offerings, etc. God's ministers have extra expenses inherent to the ministry. If you can't trust them with your money, how can you trust them with your soul?
Don't hear rumors/accusations except from two or more witnesses, and then only in front of the pastor.

II Tim. 4:2-5

Hear him as he preaches the Word.
Accept and benefit from his reproofs (**3:5-17**).

Take warning at his rebukes.
Grow under his exhorting.
Recognize the necessity of preaching:
Titus 1:3 – manifests the Word.
I Cor. 1:18, 21b – power of God, means toward salvation.
Rom. 10:13, 14 – needed for sinners to be saved.

CHAPTER 9
THE CHRISTIAN LIFE

The Christian life is so straight and narrow that only a saved person can possibly live it!

A LIFE OF RIGHTEOUSNESS

This includes doing right by God's standard, for our Saviour was altogether righteous in person and action.

Isa. 64:6

> Our personal righteousness (state and act) is unacceptable to God.
> The best we can do by ourselves when put together is nothing more than "**as filthy rags**".
> We need a righteous life produced by God (**vss. 7 and 8**).

Rom. 3:9-12

> Our best is unprofitable to God.
> Because of sin we cannot do good by God's standard.

Titus 3:5, 6

> Our personal righteousness could never save us.
> We need someone else to save us.
> We need a washing and renewing to deliver us from our own righteousness.

Titus 2:11-15

> God's grace brings salvation (**11**).
> This grace appears to **ALL** men (**11**).
> This grace teaches the saved to live righteously in this present world (**12**).
> Living righteously is possible because of
> God's salvation (**11**)
> Our denying ungodliness and worldly lusts (**12**)
> Our looking for Christ's return (**13**)
> Christ's purchase of us (**14**)
> Christ's redeeming us from all iniquity (**14**)
> Christ's purifying of us (**14**).

Rev. 19:7-9

> The saved make up the bride/wife of Christ.

The saved will make themselves ready for that great marriage day (**7**).
We will be arrayed in fine linen, clean and white – the righteousness of the saints. (This is the opposite of **Isa. 64:6** – one's personal righteousness – filthy rags). We now wear Christ's righteousness, part of the gifts that come with having received Jesus.

Matt. 22:1-14

The issue is not:
the invitation
accepting the invitation
responding and coming
The issue is the wedding garment.
It was the custom to send a wedding garment with the invitation (a picture of Christ's righteousness). The offender responded to the invitation but rejected the garment (righteousness). His judgment is necessary as will be that of all who want Heaven without the needed righteousness of Christ.

I Cor. 1:26-31

High status among men can be a hindrance to salvation. God is not impressed by who we seem to be.
God works among the humbled that He might receive the glory.
Christ is made our righteousness (**30**), and we are to live for, through, and reflecting Him.

Rom. 3:20-26

We can have and exhibit "the righteousness of God" (21, 22, 25, 26).
This righteousness comes apart from the law (**21**).
It comes "***by faith***" (**22, 26**).

James 2:21-26

True faith will produce works.
It takes faith for us to have righteousness and to be righteous.
This righteousness is "***imputed***" or put on our account by faith, yet it shows up in the work we do.

I Pet. 4:17, 18

Only the righteous are saved and that scarcely.
The unrighteous have no Biblical hope of salvation.

I John 2:29

Jesus is righteous.
Righteousness is something to be done.
Doing (ongoing, continual) righteousness is evidence of being born again.

I John 3:7

Doing righteousness is evidence of personal righteousness.
This is so for both the believer and the Saviour.

Rom. 10:1-10

The Jewish people had a lack of knowledge of God's righteousness being offered for us through Jesus by faith.
Being full of zeal they labored to establish their own righteousness.
Saving faith is of the heart and unto righteousness (Christ's). The believer will believe unto righteous living.

Rom. 6:9-13

There are three key words that unlock this chapter: know, reckon, and yield.
Once we "**know**" that our righteousness must come from and be produced by God, we should by faith reckon it to be so.
Yielding is to be to God with our personal members yielded as "*instruments of righteousness*".
We are to refuse to yield our members as "*instruments of unrighteousness unto sin*".

Rom. 6:18, 19

Through salvation we have been delivered from servitude or bondage to sin.
As we once yielded to sin in action we should now yield to righteousness in action.

Phil. 3:3-9

Paul had more reason to hope in a self-produced righteousness (**4-6**).
Paul counted his righteousness as loss and dung.
He recognized the superiority and desirability of Christ's righteousness.

SAVED AND SEPARATE FROM THE WORLD

("**World**" means the standards, way of thought, way of life of this lost generation).

THIS WORLD IS CONTROLLED BY SATAN AND DEMONS

John 12:30-32
The world is under judgment and has been since Calvary.
This world has a prince that rules over it – he was cast out back then.

John 12:47, 48
Jesus did not come to judge the world but to save it.
The judgment is accomplished by the Word – what Jesus said.

John 14:30
Satan is again given the title, "**Prince of this World**".
He has never had anything in Jesus. He operates totally apart from Christ, as does his world.

John 16:7-11
The work of the Holy Spirit involves exposing the judgment of Satan, the prince of this world.
This is to encourage sinners to lose hope in the world and turn to Jesus.

II Cor. 4:3, 4
The arch enemy of Christ and men's souls is called "**the god of this world**". He not only rules (prince) but collects all worship not given to Jesus.
He blinds the minds of sinners to keep them from Christ.

Eph. 6:12
Four realms of demonic activity are named here:
Principalities – governments of this world.
Powers – powerful segments of society in this world (i.e. education, economy, press, military etc.)
Rulers of the darkness of this world – areas opposed to righteousness and Jesus (i.e. philosophies, pornography, evolution, fear, crimes, atheism etc.)
Spiritual wickedness in high places – religion apart from that which is Biblical and of Jesus.

CHAPTER 9: THE CHRISTIAN LIFE

Believers are to be in opposition to these forces operating in and over this world.

I John 4:4

Saved people are to live in victory.
The power of the Holy Spirit is contrasted with Satan's – "**he that is in the world**".

Rev. 12:9

Satan is identified by several other titles.
He is said to deceive the whole world. This simply means that the "**world**" is deceived by Satan.
Lost are in and of this world.

Eph. 2:1, 2

The lost live in a world that controls the boundaries of their walk.
The course is established and they travel it.
Being dead in sin, they have no spiritual power or desire to escape the flow.

I John 2:2, 15-17

A love of the world is one of the evidences of being lost – without the love of God.
The world and God are contrasted:
Lust of the flesh – normal human desires for self (interior)
Lust of the eyes – desires based on

appeal through sight (exterior)

Pride of life – building up of self etc.

II Tim. 4:10

Demas is an example of loving the world.
He had to leave the company of the saved due to his love – they had nothing in common.

James 4:4

Friendship with the world is spiritual adultery.
Friendship with the world makes one the enemy of God.
Those in the world are God's enemies, not His children.

II Pet. 2:19-22

These were in the world, temporarily escaped its pollutions, and then were once again entangled in it.

Like the sow, they were washed but went back to that which was their nature.
They really never ceased to be "*world*", but only were temporarily cleansed.

I John 5:18, 19

Notice the contrast between "*we*" and "*world*" (**vs. 19**).
The world covers all who are not saved.
We are to be SAVED FROM the world.

Gal. 1:3, 4

One of the reasons Jesus gave Himself for our sins was to deliver us (rescue us) from this word (present and evil).
This is God's will in the matter of salvation.
We are to be SEPARATE from the world.

Matt. 5:14

The world is in darkness.
We are to be the opposite – light.
We are to offset the influence of the world.

Luke 16:8

Worldly wisdom differs from that of the saved.
Worldly wisdom is superior to ours – only in this generation.
Our wisdom is wiser in the light of eternity.

John 15:18, 19

We are not of the world, but rather, chosen out of the world.
The world hated Jesus and will hate us also.

John 16:33

We will not find peace in the world but tribulation.
Being separate from the world we can find peace in Jesus.

John 17:9-16 – HIGH PRIESTLY PRAYER

Jesus prayed that His followers be distinctly separate from the world.
We must live "*in the world*" but we are not "*of the world*'.
(Example of being in the water, but not of the water).
This simply follows the example of Jesus and puts us in line for answers to His praying!

CHAPTER 9: THE CHRISTIAN LIFE

Rom. 12: 1, 2

We are not to let the world press us or fashion us into its mold. We should not think, act, desire etc. like the world.

Instead of being in the world's form (or mold), we should be changed (or transformed) through mind renewal (ongoing).

Scripture and Biblical principles should govern our thinking, learning, motives, and goals.

I Cor. 4:9, 13

The world does not have the ability to properly evaluate the believer. We are too different and separate from them and their value system.

The world in prideful ignorance looks down on the saint as a spectacle, filth, and off scouring.

Titus 2:12

God's saving grace also teaches the saint necessary lessons.

We are to actively deny any and all worldly lusts (The world operates partially on a basis of lust.)

We must live right "***In this present world***". That will surely make us separated.

Heb. 11:7

Noah's obedience (faith) condemned the world.

Our obedience (faith-based) still condemns a world (sight-based) who must have proof before acting.

Heb. 11:38

The world was not worthy of the saints of the past.

The world has no reason to expect or deserve God's people today.

I John 3:1

The world never really knew Jesus.

The world can never really know the true saint. They can only know their own.

I John 3:13

The world's hatred of believers should never surprise us.

Just being saved is sufficient explanation for the world's hatred.

I John 4:5, 6

Those of the world speak of the world and are heard by the world.

God' children hear God's people.
As a rule, the world does not hear God's people. Only a few here and there will respond to the gospel.
A man or woman's audience identifies the speaker.
This is the real test of truth and error!
We are to have <u>VICTORY</u> over the world.

Gal. 6:14
We should be dead to the world and the world dead to us.
Jesus won the victory at the cross.
Jesus' crucifixion is also our victory over the world.

James 1:27
We are capable of keeping ourselves unspotted from the world.
This is one of the marks of pure religion.
This is certainly a part of .

II Pet. 1:4
We can escape the corruption of lusts that are in this world.
This is accomplished through God's promises and the change in our nature.

I John 5:4, 5
One of the marks of being born again is that we overcome (th - on a regular basis) the world.
The faith by which we are saved continues to work and give us this victory continually. This is the normal pattern of .
Our faith in the Jesus of the Bible brings deliverance and victory!
A Life of Good Works
The Need

Eph. 2:8-10
Works don't save.
Salvation by God's grace produces good works.
God works on us and changes us to show His workmanship.
He creates us in Jesus to perform good works.
God has ordained that all saved should walk in good works.
Lack of good works throws doubt on an individual's Christianity.

Matt. 16:27
Our salvation is in Jesus.

CHAPTER 9: THE CHRISTIAN LIFE

We shall be rewarded according to our works. Our works reveal our soul's condition.

Rev. 20:12, 13
The lost have all their works recorded by God.
On judgment day they will face their record.

Rev. 22:12
Jesus is coming quickly with rewards for each.
The nature of our works determines our reward.
Basic Principles

Matt. 5:16
Our light should so shine that others "**may see your good works**".
We are not to hide our good works, and certainly not to be without them.
We won't need to brag on our works – just do them in our light.
Good works out of saved sinners brings God glory.

John 14:12
We are commissioned and expected to do good works.
These works are similar to what Jesus did.
They are an evidence of genuine salvation
we continue His works here on earth.

John 17:4
Jesus had a particular amount (and kind) of work to do.
It was possible to do this work in the time allotted.
Jesus finished His work.
Do we know ours? Will we complete it before we go home?

II Tim. 4:7
Paul had a certain course to complete – a given amount of work to do.
He finished his before going home.
Are we on course or off?

I Cor. 3:13-15
Our work(s) will be judged as to quality. The test will be by fire.
Some shall be rewarded, others will suffer loss/smoke/ashes.

I Cor. 15:58

We are to abound in good works – aim for the maximum, not minimum.
Doctrinally and practically we are to be stable, solid, and not moved.
Inconsistency decreases our usefulness.
Work done in the Lord is never wasted or vain.

II Cor. 6:1

Good works are not performed in isolation.
We operate in a partnership
with others
with the Lord.

II Cor. 9:8

We not only are to perform good works, but "*every*" good work – variety.
God's grace provides a sufficiency to be able to accomplish these – abounding.

Phil. 2:12, 13

Our works are the result of God working in us.
God works both on our will and in empowering our ability to do.

I Tim. 5:25

All good works shall be shown.
This is not our responsibility – God has His own timing.
Some are shown soon but the others will be revealed later.
You cannot permanently hide good works.

II Tim. 2:15

Bible study prepares us for works.
God's approval opens doors of opportunity.
We can so work that we have no reason to be ashamed before God.

II Tim. 2:21

Purging ourselves prepares us for "*every good work*":
vs. 4 – entangled with the affairs of this life
vs. 5 – dishonest striving
vs. 6 – laziness
vs. 13 – unbelief
vs. 14 – foolish striving
vs. 16 – profane and vain babblings

CHAPTER 9: THE CHRISTIAN LIFE

vs. 18 – error
vs. 22 – youthful lusts
vs. 23 – foolish and unlearned questions
We should be concerned with honor, sanctification, God's standards met, preparation for good works.

II Tim. 3:16, 17

Scriptures furnish the man of God unto good works.
Scriptures are adequate to completely prepare for "**all**" good works.

Titus 2:14

Christ's sacrifice of Himself was to prepare us for good works.
This involves redemption from all iniquity, making us unique, and producing zeal.

Titus 3:8, 14

Believers are to be constantly reminded of the need for good works.
We must take special care to be consistent and maintain such works.
Works should be in necessary areas – not in nonessentials.
Works are related to fruit.

James 2:14-26

What value is there in a faith that produces no good works? A tree without fruit? A life unchanged by God?
Absence of works is evidence of a dead faith.
The evidence of faith is its fruit of good works. No fruit means there is no faith to be seen.
Demons have faith enough to tremble, but they are not saved, – still are demons. You can tell by their lack of good works.
(**22**) Works are the completion of genuine faith. They show up in the life of true believers.

Rev. 14:13

The saved labor and have works.
We never are separated from these – they follow us past death.

Rev. 2:2, 5, 9, 13, 19, 23, 26; 3:1, 8, 15

Works were a constant issue in the last message of Jesus to the churches.
Churches should keep works in their focus.
Types of Good Works (Acts called "good works" in the Bible)

John 6:28, 29
Belief on Jesus is a good work.
Trusting Him is essential.

Acts 9:36-39
Clothing of needy widows.
Issue of pure religion (**James 1:27**).

Acts 26:20
Repentance produces fruit or good works.
Seven are named in **II Cor. 7:11.**

I Cor. 9:1
Spiritual children are a good work.
Seeing sinners converted takes work.

I Thess. 1:3
Faith is a work – it requires resisting flesh and logic plus following the Scriptures (**II Thess. 1:11**)
Love takes labor – it isn't always easy.

I Tim. 3:1
The pastorate is a good work.
The pastorate takes much work – spiritually, intellectually, emotionally, physically.

I Tim. 5:10
Raising children.
Lodging strangers.
Faithful to communion.
Relieving the afflicted.

I Tim. 6:17-19
Distribute financially to others.
Open to the needs of others.

II Tim. 4:5
Evangelism.
We should labor to reach souls.

Titus 2:7, 8
kept without corruption.
Men be grave and sincere.

CHAPTER 9: THE CHRISTIAN LIFE

Speech kept correct, accurate, clear, and on proper subjects.

Heb. 13:21

All those areas that make up the will of God for us.
Living "well-pleasing in His sight".
A Life of Truth

John 18:38

Pilate pictures the lost man.
He is never sure what truth is.

John 14:6

Declares Himself to be truth.
In Him there is no error or lie.

John 16:13

The Holy Spirit is called the Spirit of truth.
He always operated from a basis of truth.

I John 4:5, 6

Our lives and speech are to be under the control of the Spirit of truth.
This separates us from the world.

I John 5:6

The Spirit being truth is the basis for His being the witness.
This is why we can trust the inner witness of the Spirit.

I John 2:27

The Spirit's being truth is the basis for His teaching ministry.
The Spirit's teaching can always be trusted to be truth.

John 17:17

God's Word is truth.
Our lives should demonstrate the Scriptures. They should be lived, not simply read and known.

II Tim. 2:15

The Bible is called the Word of Truth.
It is to be studied, incorporated into our lives, and rightly divided.

James 1:18

Our second birth was produced by the Word of Truth.

will reveal its origins.

John 1:14
Christ's life was full of truth.
Our lives should reflect Christ's.

John 1:17
Jesus brought grace and truth.
The evidence of real grace is usually a life of truth.

John 3:15-21
Truth is not to be confined to the intellect, but put into action. All truth is to be lived.
Fully doing truth requires God's working in our lives. It shows the contrast of saved and lost.

John 8:32
Truth frees us.
Our degree of freedom is based on our receptivity of truth.

John 8:40-46
Truth telling is a mark of Jesus.
Lying is a mark of Satan.
Followers carry the mark of their leader.

Rom. 3:6-8
Lying brings judgment.
The end <u>never</u> justifies the means.
Those who think anything less than the truth will be used of God are under a curse of damnation.

II Cor. 4:1, 2
We should renounce all dishonesty, craftiness, and deceitfulness.
We should live to show the truth to all.

II Cor. 11:10
The truth of Christ is to be in us.
This truth should move us to action.

Gal. 4:16
We should tell the truth even if we lose friends and gain enemies.
Any that become enemies over the truth have an enormous problem – with God truth, logic, honesty, morality, and spirituality.

CHAPTER 9: THE CHRISTIAN LIFE

Eph. 4:15
Truth is to be spoken on a regular basis.
Truth is to be spoken in love.
This is one of the products of a proper church.

Eph. 4:25
Lying is not for Christians.
Lying doesn't disappear on its own, but rather must be put away.
Truthfulness is related to our unity as Christians.

Eph. 5:9
The Holy Spirit indwells all believers.
The Holy Spirit produces fruit in our lives.
One aspect of this fruit is truth. No truth means no fruit of the Spirit.

Eph. 6:14
We are to wear armour for protection in the spiritual warfare with Satan.
Different parts of our being/spiritual body are protected by different aspects of .
The first named piece to put on is truth.
This protects very sensitive areas of our being.
No protection (no truth) and there will be great pain, defeat, and possible inability to produce other Christians. Little protection makes for suffering and limitations.

II Thess. 2:10-12
The lost will perish because "**they received not the love of the truth**". The truth is to be loved as well as believed.
Those who have pleasure in unrighteousness (the opposite of truth) will believe a lie.

I Tim. 2:4
Truth is to be known – a realm of knowledge.
God desires that all men come to this knowledge.
One must be saved to come to this knowledge.

I Tim. 4:2-3
Truth is to be believed.
Truth will free us from doctrines of devils:
lying

hypocrisy
seared conscience
celibacy
vegetarianism
Truth will keep us from departing from the faith.

I Tim. 6:5

Philosophy that prosperity is evidence of godliness is empty of the truth.
We are to remove or withdraw ourselves from those who believe such:
they have corrupt minds
their arguments are perverse
they are destitute of all the truth

II Tim. 3:7

For some the process of learning never leads to the product of knowledge of the truth.
This is a particular peril in the last days – learning but never really knowing.

II Tim. 4:4

The choice to turn from the truth leads to believing fables.
They turn themselves at first, – then they <u>are</u> <u>turned</u>.
We must never turn from any truth God shows us.

James 3:14-16

Envying and strife evidence a life out of tune with the truth.
When envy and strife are defended, the source of logic is not heavenly but:
earthly
sensual
devilish
Envy and strife bring with them confusion, and lead to any and every evil work.
God's wisdom is contrasted:
pure
peaceable
gentle
easy to be entreated
full of mercy
full of good fruits

CHAPTER 9: THE CHRISTIAN LIFE

without partiality
without hypocrisy
A life of truth will reflect God's wisdom

James 5:12

A life of truth requires always telling the truth.
Those that must swear to tell the truth evidence the likelihood of telling falsehoods when not under oath.
God's people need no oath. We should always tell the truth.

I John 1:6, 8

Truth is not only to be known but also done. All truth is practical.
<u>Doing</u> <u>the</u> <u>truth</u> involves walking in light and not darkness.
Doing the truth involves being in fellowship with God. He always walks in the light because He is light.
Truth is to reside within us.
Truth is to be so clear and strong that sin is exposed in us.
Truth will constantly show us our fallen condition and the law of sin within.
Any who would even say they have no sin are without this truth that would expose them to themselves.

I John 2:4

Truth residing within will bring us to obey Christ's commandments.
Lack of exterior obedience is evidence of no truth within.
Denial of sin or lack of obedience to commandments is the very opposite of the truth of God.

I John 2:21

God's Word is addressed primarily to the saved; they know the truth.
Saved know that lies are unrelated to the truth.
Sanctity of the Home

(This is dealt with at greater length and detail in "*Framework for Families*")

Husband-Wife Relationship

Eph. 5:22

This is God's will (**vs. 17**).
Wives are to be in submission to their own husbands, – no one else's.

Submission is active, not passive or fatalistic. Wives can protest wrong, and are no longer responsible when obedience is still required.

Eph. 5:23, 24

Christ's headship of the Church is the example for the home.
The Church's submission teaches couples how to operate in the home.
Husbands are to give commands in wisdom even as Jesus does.
Submission pattern is protection in both O. T. and N. T.:
Numbers 30:1-15
I Cor. 11:3
I Tim. 2:12-14

Eph. 5:25

Husbands are required to love their wives.
This love is both sacrificial and selfless.

Eph. 5:31

Married men are to leave home.
The marriage union makes us one in God's eyes.

I Pet. 3:1

The wife's submission is so thorough that it is called subjection.
Subjection is a powerful tool to bring a husband in line with the Word of God, and even bring a lost one to Jesus.

I Pet. 3:2

The life must be holy and pure.
The heart must fear God and sin.

I Pet. 1:3, 4

The adorning to reach a husband is not outwardly for the senses, but from within.
Such an adornment is not only hard to come by but also costly to maintain. Trials and persecution will be used to test its reality.

I Pet. 1:5, 6

Sarah is God's example of submission!
Others have found that God protects submissive wives.
Obey your husband, trust God, and don't be afraid.

CHAPTER 9: THE CHRISTIAN LIFE

I Pet. 1:7

Husbands are to have the right knowledge to qualify for marriage.
They are to honor their wives.
They must be right in this relationship lest their prayer-life be handicapped.

I Tim. 3:2-7

Pastors are to have one wife.
They are to rule well in their homes.
They are to have their children under control.

I Tim. 3:8-12

Deacons also are to have one wife.
They must rule their own homes and children.
Their wives must meet certain qualifications.

I Tim. 5:8

God expects a man to provide for his family.
Lack of provision is a denial of Christianity and a supplying Christ.

I Tim. 5:14, 15

Younger women are to marry and bear children.
While the husband is the head of the home, the wife is to guide the house. This speaks of the balance of authority. It also speaks of staying home and not running around (**vs. 13**).

Titus 2:1-8

Four groups are mentioned with specific instructions for each:
aged men (**vs. 2**)
aged women (**vs. 3**)
young women (**vs. 4**)
young men (**vs. 6**).
The older are to teach and set a pattern for the younger.
The young women are to stay in the home caring for and loving their husbands and children.
The young men are to be responsible, serious-minded, providing for their families.

Gen. 3:16-19

The curse from sin established certain family relationships.
The wife is to bear the children and be in submission to the husband.

The husband is to provide for the family by working with great effort and suffering.

Neither wives nor husbands are to avoid their responsibilities

Prov. 31:10-31

A virtuous woman will find sufficient freedom to operate within the home structure to care for their husband
and children as well as help with family finances.

A right wife is an asset, but a shameful one will weaken a man (**12:4**).

I Cor. 7:1, 2

Touching (other than a brief handshake) by men and women (other than husband and wife) is not good nor wise.

Such is for those who are married or about to be so.

This serves as a barrier to petting which leads to fornication.

I Cor. 7:10, 11

Divorce and remarriage were forbidden by Jesus.

These verses are a summation of the Gospel teaching:

Matt. 5:31, 32
Matt. 19:3-9
Mark 10:1-12
Luke 16:18.

I Cor. 7:12-16

Issue of unequal yokes dealt with.

Such were not to be knowingly entered into (**II Cor. 6:14**), but what do you do when you find yourself in one?

Believer is not to leave by choice.

Believer does not have to keep the unbeliever from leaving.

Believer does not have to receive the departed unbeliever back again.

Perhaps the believer can reach the unbeliever and see them saved.

I Cor. 7:27-34

There is a state of blessed singleness.

The unmarried are freer to serve the Lord.

I Cor. 7:38-40

Only death ends a marriage.

CHAPTER 9: THE CHRISTIAN LIFE

After the death of a spouse, it is permissible to marry again, tho it is not always advisable.
Proper Training of Children (Good results can be had.)

II Tim. 1:5

Timothy had a genuine faith.
This came from his home and influence of mother and grandmother.

II Tim. 3:15

The Holy Scriptures can be taught and known from childhood.
The foundation for salvation should be laid.

Luke 2:41-47, 52

Jesus could talk with the best Bible scholars of His day when He was only 12-years of age.
He grew in wisdom – therefore we are looking at His human side! Consider the implications of His home life and the home life of our children.
Other children were well trained before adulthood (Dan. 1:3, 4, 8; Jer. 1:7; I Sam. 17:33; II Sam. 3:1-4; Gen. 37:2).
Means Must Be Used To Train

Deut. 6:4-12

Daily instruction in the Bible is needed ... family devotions are a part of this.
Proper examples by the parents are needed.

Psm. 78:1-8

Bible truths learned from other generations are to be passed on to younger generations.
This teaching is not only to teach but also to prepare students to become teachers of teachers. This will set up a perpetual line of teaching and learning.
This teaching is to include God's praises, strength, and wonderful work (**vs. 4**); His testimony and law (**vs. 5**).
It should produce improved saints even more holy than previous generations (**vss. 7 and 8**).

Prov. 22:6

Each child is different and needs a different path in specifics, though the same in general.

Parents should know that course and how to train each child according to God's plan for that child.
God guarantees the product is tied to the process.

Eph. 6:1-4
Fathers bear the primary responsibility for spiritual instruction of the children.
Two areas are expected: nurture – the feeding, encouraging, instructing, helping; and admonition – warning, correcting, setting limits, showing dangers, stimulating to right choices and actions.

Matt. 15:22-28
Bring children with difficulties to Jesus for help. Know the problem, know where and to whom to take them, and plead their case.
Either father or mother has the authority to bring son or daughter (**Mark 9:17-24**).
They can also be brought to Jesus for blessings (**Mark 10:13-16**).
Discipline Must Be Biblical

Prov. 22:6
Training is "**up**" while their nature pulls downward; therefore, there will be tension and struggle.
The child must learn the boundaries permitted in the way they are to go, and not be going beyond these boundaries.

Prov. 13:24
Love produces discipline.
Lack of spanking is evidence of hatred of the child.
The instrument to be used is the rod.

Prov. 19:18
Spanking is normally needed from time to time.
Don't let their crying keep you from your responsibility. God promises inward change through this means (**20:30**).

Prov. 22:15
Foolishness is natural in children and is actually bound in the heart.
The rod of correction can drive it out and far from him.
The rod is for correction, not punishment. It is to be used to bring improved behavior.

Prov. 23:13, 14
Children are headed to hell and by nature will continue on this path.

The rod well applied can change the path and deliver the soul from hell.
Many children of saved parents will go to hell because Biblical discipline was neglected or resisted.

Prov. 29:15-17

Lack of Biblical discipline will bring shame on the parents in later life when it is too late to correct the matter.
Proper discipline produces rest and delight for the parents in later life.

SETTLING OF PERSONAL DIFFERENCES

Between Christians

I John 4:19-5:2

Christians will love one another for this is our nature.
This love will be revealed by love for God and obedience to His commands.

I Cor. 13:4-7

Christian love will manifest itself by the 15 virtues here named.
Lack of any of these virtues shows a defective love. This in itself will help us get to the root of many differences, – a lack of love.

Rom. 12:9, 10, 14

Love should be genuine and without hypocrisy or play-acting.
We should hate and shun evil.
We should cling to what is good.
We should have love gently toward each other.
We should give honor to others and see that they get the preferential position.
When we are mistreated we should bless our persecutors.

Rom. 12:17-21

Evil in others is no excuse for us to respond with evil (**17**).
Deceit is not helpful in solving problems (**17**).
We should aim to live peaceably with all men. It is not always possible, but it is desirable.
God can punish, avenge, and even any scores that need to be dealt with.
We should learn to show kindness even to our enemies.
Good is stronger than evil and should be used to overcome evil.

Matt. 5:22-24

Causeless anger with a brother is wrong.
The degree of it may reveal such inner sin that will bring judgment upon us one day **or** be evidence of an unregenerate heart.
If our brother has anything against us we should seek reconciliation. This is of higher importance and priority than giving or praying! (**Prov. 18:19**).

Matt. 18:15-18

If we have something against our brother we are to seek him out and try to resolve it.
Failure to resolve it should be followed by a second visit with a witness, and then the church discussion if need be.
Refusal to resolve is likely evidence of being lost.

I Cor. 6:1-8

Christians should not take Christians to court to recover finances.
It is better to lose the money than losing the brother, losing your testimony and placing yourself in jeopardy before lost judges.
Saints are better qualified to judge matters than the lost judges – we are in training to judge greater matters.
We not only will judge the world but also angels.
Matters of this life should be able to be sorted out by the least esteemed in the church.
It is wrong to defraud your brother.
It is better to be defrauded by a Christian than grudge or go to court. **Vss. 9-10** show the condition of rebellious, defrauding, covetous people.

With the Lost

Matt. 5:38-48

(**40**) If you lose a lawsuit, pay off.
(**42**) Don't be stingy. Help the needy. Loan to those with equity.
(**44**) A Christian attitude towards the lost is the opposite of the world's response.
(**48**) Our pattern is our Father.
Vengeance is His area as is blessing, and He will balance all things.

A Life of Prayer

Jesus taught the disciples "*to pray*" and not "*to preach*".

CHAPTER 9: THE CHRISTIAN LIFE

Perhaps as much as 1/3 of Jesus' teaching had to do with prayer.
A believer's prayer life is the best indicator of his spiritual condition. Prayer is one place where the sovereignty of God and the responsibility of man meet! Often as we pray God exercises His sovereignty.

Phil. 4:6

Requests are to be made known to God.
All areas of life are open to prayer and should be prayed about.

I Thess. 5:17

Prayer should be at all times.
We should be constantly in communion with our God.
We should never give up on praying.
We should persevere with our requests until rejected.

Luke 18:1

The meaning of the parable is given before the parable – a most unusual occurrence.
Jesus emphasized the need for constant prayer.
The alternative to prayer is fainting and vice versa.

I John 1:3-7

One of the marks of eternal life is fellowship with God.
No communion with God is evidence of being lost.

Matt. 7:7

The way of progress is governed by prayer.
We must ask to receive, ask to find, and knock to have things opened for us.

Rom. 8:34, 26

The Son of God intercedes.
We are to be conformed to His image; therefore we are to become intercessors.
The Holy Spirit assists us in this ministry (**vs. 26**) by helping us and by making intercession for us.

Eph. 6:18

Prayer is basic to the spiritual warfare (**vss. 10-19**).
Constant prayer in all forms and areas with supplications are vital resources of power.

Rom. 1:9

We should pray for each other as Christians.
This is part of our serving Christ.
This type praying should never cease; it is always needed.

I Cor. 1:4

We should also thank God constantly for other Christians.
God's grace in them should stir us to praise.
Practical love and growing faith in our brethren ought to motivate our thanking God (**II Thess. 1:3**).

Acts 12:5

Peter was delivered because of prayer.
The church chose this weapon rather than resorting to other methods.

I Sam. 12:23

Ceasing to pray can be sin against God!
We are under a divine obligation to pray for our brethren.

Acts 6:2-4

We are to guard against anything which hinders our prayer life.
Praying is ranked with ministry of the Word – precedes it in order and priority.

Col. 4:2;-4

Prayer can open doors for the Gospel.
Prayer may determine the clarity and power of the message of the Gospel.

II Thess. 3:1-2

Prayer may determine the reception of the Gospel.
Prayer can determine the safety of the preachers of the Gospel.
Evidencing the Fruit of the Spirit

Gal. 5:19-21

Works of the flesh are in contrast with the fruit of the Spirit (**vs. 22**).
Works of the flesh are evidence of an unconverted soul.

CHAPTER 9: THE CHRISTIAN LIFE

Gal. 5:22-23

Fruit of the Spirit contrasts and shows the work of conversion – what the Holy Spirit produces.

Singular fruit has nine sides, aspects, identities, etc.

Love, joy, peace are graces of inward character. They operate within but radiate outwardly.

Longsuffering, gentleness and goodness are resultant outward graces of character expressed toward others.

Faith, meekness and temperance are expressions of heart shown towards God and observed by others.

These are nine normal areas produced as fruit by the indwelling Holy Spirit. The flesh will strive against these (**vs. 17**) but we are to walk in the Spirit (**vss. 16, 25**). We must crucify the flesh (**vs. 24**), not pamper, provide for, or excuse it.

Gal. 2:20

Our life is not our own to do with as we please.

We are to let Christ live through and in us.

He has purchased us and provided faith for living with HIM in control.

John 15:1-17

A mark of discipleship is fruit production (**vs. 8**).

Fruit comes in varying quantities:

fruit (**vs. 2**)

more fruit (**vs. 2**)

much fruit (**vss. 5, 8**).

The vital union of the vine with the branches is evidenced by the production of fruit.

We've been ordained:

to go

bring forth fruit

have fruit that lasts.

Love and joy are mentioned in the context of fruit (**vss. 9-13, 17**).

I Cor. 13:1-13

The marks of charity (practical love) are clearly seen.

This is placing the fruit of the Spirit in the midst of the gifts of the Spirit (**chapters 12 and 14**). The gifts without the fruit are unprofitable (**vs. 1-3**).

II John 1:6

> The fruit of the Spirit – love – has practical and observable outworkings.
> Biblical or Spirit-produced love shows in the life and walk of the believer-obedience to the Scriptures (**I John 2:3, 4**).

I John 2:9, 10

> Biblical love brings a walk in the light.
> Biblical love will give no occasion of stumbling to a brother.

I John 2:15-17

> Spirit-produced love will not produce a love of the world.
> Nor of the things in the world.

I John 3:1

> This fruit of love is bestowed upon us, not worked up.
> One result is the world cannot know/understand us.

I John 3:11-18

> We should be ready to die for the brethren.
> We should share with these brethren who have real needs.

I John 4:7-5:3

> Love is an evidence of knowing God (**4:7**).
> Love is evidence of the indwelling fruit-producing Holy Spirit (**4:12, 13**).
> Spirit-produced love will give us boldness in the Day of Judgment (**4:17**).
> Love for the brethren is the evidence of love for God (**4:20, 21**).
> Love keeps God's commandments from being grievous (**5:3**).

The fruit of the Spirit produces such change of character in believers as to enable them to live and to show the life of Christ to a sin-cursed generation.

CHAPTER 10
FUTURE THINGS

Future of the Lost

John 3:15-20
>Will perish
>Already condemned

John 3:36
>God's wrath is already on them

Rom. 3:23
>Already short of God's glory
>Failures in their purpose on earth

Rom. 5:8-10
>Enemies of God

Rom. 6:23
>Death is certain – not physical but spiritual

Luke 16:22, 23
>Hell
>Torments

Luke 16:24
>Body in the grave (**22**)
>Soul in Hell suffers pain from flames before resurrection

Luke 16:25
>Memory continues
>Contrast of earth and Hell understood

Luke 16:26
>No escape possible
>No help able to come

Luke 16:27-31
>Spiritual concerns without ability or opportunity to obtain mercy
>Inability to help family etc. still back on earth

Understand need for repentance but unable to repent

Isa. 33:14
Devouring fire
Everlasting burnings

II Thess. 1:9
Place of punishment
Everlasting destruction
> No grace or mercy – the Lord's presence and glory of His power are destroyed from them

Rev. 14:10, 11
Drink of the wine of the wrath of God
Tormented with fire and brimstone
Smoke of torment ascends forever and ever
No end of suffering or annihilation
No rest

Rev. 20:1
Pit without bottom
Falling but never landing

Rev. 20:6
First resurrection is only for the saved
Second death is for the lost

Rev. 20:11-15
Second resurrection brings all the lost to the Great White Throne.
Second death is defined as the lake of fire with death and Hell cast in it.
Lost judged for works
destiny is Hell
destiny is certain
issue is degree of suffering

Rev. 22:10, 11
Unjust will stay unjust
Filthy will stay filthy
Death does not improve the character or actions of the lost.

Rev. 22:15
Lost are excluded from God's city.

CHAPTER 10: FUTURE THINGS

They followed error rather than Jesus, the Truth.
They will be mixed with dogs (sodomites), sorcerers, immoral, murderers, and idolaters for the rest of eternity.
Future of the Saved

John 14:1-6
Mansions
Place prepared
Jesus is coming again
We shall be with Jesus

I Thess. 4:13-18
Ever with the Lord
Caught up to Jesus

I Thess. 5:9
Not appointed to wrath (of God)
Will suffer persecution of man

Rev. 4:1-11
Picture of the rapture (**1, 2**)
Throne
See who is on the Throne (**2, 3**)
Twenty-four elders (**4**)
Holy Spirit (**5**)
Four Beasts (**6-8**)
Worship (**9-11**)
Purpose of Creation

Rev. 5:8-13
Vials of prayer (**8**)
Stored in Heaven
New Song (**9-10**)
Reigning
Angels beyond counting (**11**)
Lamb is Worthy (**12**)
Creation praises Jesus (**13**)

Heb. 9:27
Death for all (saved and lost)
Judgment after death

Rom. 14:10-12

Believers face the Judgment Seat of Christ.
We shall give an account
of ourselves
to God

II Cor. 5:10-12

All believers appear at Judgment Seat of Christ.
Every one receives according to what has been done.
good
bad
Terror of the Lord exists and motivates us to persuade men.
We are manifest to God.
We desire to be manifest to saints' consciences.
Glory not in appearances but in changes of heart.

I Cor. 3:9-15

Three pictures (**9**)
Laborers together
God's husbandry
God's building
How we build is as important as with what we build (**10**)
Jesus is the foundation (**11**)
Quality, not quantity, determines what lasts (**12-15**).
Judgment is not for destiny but for rewards.

Rev. 19:1-6

Heaven is a place of praise.
We will rejoice over judgment of "***the great whore***" who killed the saints.

Rev. 19:7-9

Marriage Supper of the Lamb is for the bride (wife)
Special garments for the saints

Rev. 19:11-21

Jesus will come in glory.
Jesus comes to rule the nations with the rod of iron.
Christ's armies come with Him in fine linen, clean and white.
Supper of the great God
Christ's enemies fully defeated
Beast and false prophet are cast alive into the lake of fire.

CHAPTER 10: FUTURE THINGS

Rev. 20:1-9

Satan put in bottomless pit for 1000 years.
Thousand year period (6 times in 7 verses).
Reigning, Thrones, Priests
Fickle citizens will still follow Satan to attack the saints.

Rev. 20-10-15

Satan cast into Lake of Fire
Saints are forever with Jesus
We will witness the judgment of the lost at the Great White Throne.

Rev. 21:1, 2

New Heaven, New earth
Holy City comes out of Heaven
Former things pass away

Rev. 21:22-27

Father and Son become our Temple
Glory of God and Lamb are our light
Nations of saved
Nations of the earth
Brief Outline of Things to Come

I Thess. 4:13-18

Jesus comes in the air for His saints.
Dead saints come with Jesus and are reunited with their bodies.
Live saints are caught up to be with Jesus
Comforting truth

I Thess. 5:9

Saints are appointed to salvation not wrath.
Lost are appointed to wrath not salvation.

II Thess. 2:7-12

Mystery of Iniquity that now works is hindered but will one day be released from restrictions
The controller of the Mystery of Iniquity will be taken out of the way.
This removal leads to the revelation of a particular "**wicked**" one
To be dealt with later by the Lord at His coming
Operates by Satan's working
power, signs, lying wonders

deceiving the lost
No second chance for those who received not the love of the truth

Rev. 6:7-17

God's judgments on mankind on the planet earth
Saints with God in Heaven
Believers martyred on earth
God's great wrath poured out

Rev. 7:14

Time of great tribulation
Salvation is still thru the blood of Jesus.

Rev. 19:11-20

Jesus coming to earth
Comes in glory victory, and destruction of His enemies.
Beast and false prophet are two separate individuals but share the same destiny.

Rev. 20:1-3

Satan – the third of the unholy, counterfeit trinity is judged
Sentence is for one thousand years

Rev. 20:4-6

Jesus rules for one thousand years.
Saints rule with Jesus

Rev. 20:7-10

Satan is loosed
Those ruled over rebel with Satan
God smashes the rebellion

Rev. 20:11-15

The Great White Throne Judgment
At this point all saints are alive (first resurrection) and all lost are dead.

Rev. 21:1

Rest of eternity is entered
Great changes occur
Brief Outline of Revelation

CHAPTER 10: FUTURE THINGS

Rev. 1:19
>Hast seen (past)
>Which are (present)
>Which shall be hereafter (future)
>Chapter 1 – past
>Chapters 2-3 – present
>Chapters 4-22 – future
>scenes in Heaven
>scenes on earth
>Occasional flashbacks and look-aheads are found for sake of clarity and perspective
>General Principles

The closer the event, the clearer the vision

Rev. 1:1
>Revelation is of Jesus
>Future has to do with Jesus at work

Rev. 19:10
>Testimony of Jesus is the spirit of prophecy
>Right prophetic teaching is Christ centered – not event, man, or nation centered.

ALWAYS USE THAT WHICH IS OPEN AND CLEAR IN ORDER TO UNDERSTAND WHAT IS CLOSED OR DIFFICULT.

Heb. 1:1, 2
>The last days started when Jesus was on earth (2000 years ago!)
>God now speaks thru Jesus

Matt. 24:1-3
>Olivet Discourse (**chapters 24, 25**) had a background setting of the Temple and its coming destruction
>Three questions are asked by the disciples and answered by the Lord:
>When shall these things be?
>What shall be the sign of thy coming?
>What shall be the sign of the end of the world?

II Pet. 1:20, 21
>No prophetic passage is to be isolated from others in its interpretation.

God has given a full revelation to be taken in its fullness.

I Tim. 4:1-6
In the latter times, some shall depart or leave the faith.
Seducing spirits will counterfeit the Holy Spirit in leading people away.
Doctrines of devils will lure people away, i.e.:
lies
hypocrisy
seared consciences
forbidding proper marriage
vegetarianism

II Tim. 3:1-14
The last days will be full of spiritual, moral, and attitude peril.
Religion will flourish but without the purity and power of God.

I John 2:18
There is a distinction between ...
antichrist – to come
antichrists – already here
Last time is marked by a singular antichrist prophesied of

II Peter 3:3-14
Last days produce scoffers
Last days produce those who walk according to their lusts (desires and feelings).
Questioning promise of Jesus coming and changing things
Willing ignorance of past changes
Next judgment of the earth will be by fire
Our relationship to Jesus is far more important than acquisition of things (they will all perish).

Rev. 22:7
Jesus' return will be quick and sudden.
There will be blessings for those who are obedient.

Rev. 22:12
Suddenness of return is repeated
Jesus brings rewards for faithful laborers.

Rev. 22:20
Suddenness is certainty

We should pray for His return.

TERMS OFFEN USED

Millennium — 1000 years of rule by Jesus

Pre-Millennium — Jesus comes before the millennium and sets up His rule

Post-Millennium — Jesus comes after we set up the Kingdom for Him

Amillennial — No millennium, the Kingdom is not physical but spiritual and on-going

Rapture — The catching up of Christians to meet Jesus in the air

Partial Rapture — Only the faithful saints are caught up

Second Coming — The return of Jesus to earth

Tribulation — Time of God's judgment on the earth with Israel a nation in their land

These terms help us understand differing views on future things

REASONS FOR A PRE-MILLENNIAL, PRE-TRIBULATIONAL RAPTURE

There is a distinction between the Rapture and the Second Coming in glory

I Thess. 4:13-18

The Lord comes in the air and we go up to meet Him (**16, 17**)
The saved dead are resurrected
Comforting truth

Zech. 14:3-9

The Lord comes to earth.
The Lord battles the nations of the earth.
Geographical changes in Israel
The Lord to be "King over all the earth"

Rev. 19:11-16
> The Lord comes to battle His enemies.
> Saints come with the Lord from Heaven as armies (**14, 7, 8**)
> Result is "the supper of the great God" (17-21)

Matt. 14:27-31
> Returns "after the tribulation" (29)
> Saints gathered by angels
> Public return with tribes of the earth mourning and nature affected
> Similar to passages in **Zech. 14** and **Rev. 19**, but different from **I Thess. 4**

DANIEL'S VISION OF 70-WEEKS

Dan. 9:24-27
> 70-weeks mentioned
> Divided 7, 62, and 1

PRINCIPLE OF TEMPORARY SUSPENSION OF RELATIONSHIP

I Kings 6:1
> Solomon started building temple in his fourth year as King.
> Temple started 480-years after Israelites left Egypt

Acts 13:18-21
> Time of Israelites after leaving Egypt is stated by segments.
> 40-years in the wilderness (**18**)
> 40-years with King Saul
> 40-years under King David
> 3-years of Solomon before the Temple (**21**)
> Total of 573-years from leaving Egypt till start of the Temple
> This makes a 93-year difference in the two passages
> God never contradicts Himself
> What truth is hidden behind these two figures?

Judges 3:8	8-years bondage
Judges 3:14	18-years bondage
Judges 4:3	20-years bondage
Judges 6:1	7-years bondage
Judges 13:1	40-years bondage

> Total of 93-years God gave Israelites over their enemies

CHAPTER 10: FUTURE THINGS

Thus, God suspended His relationship with Israel for the difference in the figures of the two passages.

BEGINNING OF THE 70-WEEKS

Dan. 9:25, 26

Seventy weeks have a specific date of starting.
The seven and sixty-two weeks have a specific date of ending.

Neh. 2:1-6

Date of starting event is established historically
Specific fulfillment of prophecy
445 BC – 1st of Nissan
Weeks figure to weeks of years

Dan. 9:24-27

Various prophecies to be fulfilled in detail
Contrast "*Messiah the Prince*" (25) and "*prince*" (26)
"**Messiah be cut off**" and "**prince that shall come**" (26) are different times on the earth
"People of the prince" – destroy (26)
"Desolations are determined" (26)
70th week and covenant (**27**)
"midst of the week" (27)
"sacrifice and oblation" (27)
Evidently sanctuary (Temple) destroyed after 69th week but operating during the 70th week
Church and Israel - different

-ORIGIN

Gen. 12:1-3

Start of Israelites
Begins with Abraham

Matt. 16:18

Church started, built, and owned by Jesus
This is a contrast with the start of Israel

Rom. 7:1-6

Death changes relationships
Jesus' death made us dead to the law to be married to Jesus.
Contrast of law and Jesus, Israel and the Church

Rom. 11:13-25

Gentiles are the wild olive branches grafted in to replace natural branches – Israel (**17**)

Unbelief brought their breaking off; faith brought our being grafted in (**20**)

The Church (mainly Gentiles) is grafted in due to Israel's blindness (**vs. 25**) and for a limited time till "**the fullness of the Gentiles be come in**".

CONTRAST ISRAEL (WIFE OF GOD) AND CHURCH (BRIDE OF CHRIST)

Isa. 54:5-8

God declares Himself as Israel's husband
God showed mercy to them

Jer. 3:1-18

Sinfulness of Israel compared to playing the harlot when married to God.
Bill of divorcement given by God to Israel (**8**)
Though divorced, yet still married and should return to God

Ezek. 16:32, 38

Israel as the wife
Israel sinning morally by spiritual wandering (**10-17**)
Israel as a spiritual harlot while the wife of God (**26-32**)
Israel to come back to God in shame for her sin (**60-63**)

Hosea 2

Israel left God for Balaam (**13**)
Likened to adulterous Gomer leaving Hosea
God will woo Israel back (**14-23**)

Hosea 3:1-5

Israel who has left God will return in the latter days
This will occur after doing without a King, prince, or sacrifice

Eph. 5:22-32

Marriage pictures the relationship of Jesus and the Church (**23**)
Church to be subject to Christ (**24**)
Christ's love of the Church is pattern for husbands towards wives (**25**)

Marriage teaching is primarily teaching of Christ and the Church (**32**)

Rev. 19:7-9
Jesus is the Lamb
The wife would be the Church
The marriage supper is coming one day

-TYPES IN GENESIS

Abraham	God	Gen. 12-25
Sarah	Israel	Gen. 12-23
Isaac	Jesus	Gen. 21, 22
Eliezer	Holy Spirit	Gen. 24
Rebekah	Church	Gen. 24
Keturah	Israel restored	Gen. 25

TEACHING IN ACTS

Acts 1:6-8
Disciples focus on restoring Israel then
Times and Seasons in the Father's power
Disciples to refocus on reaching the whole world

Acts 2: 5, 22
Message to audience of leaders of Israel
Jesus had come to Israel and they rejected Him

Acts 2:46
Early Church met in Temple
Israel's leaders rejected Church for meeting at the Temple.

Acts 8:5, 14
Gospel taken beyond Israel to Samaria
Church recognized this as proper

Acts 10:28
Gospel moves on to Gentiles
God shows there is now a change (**34, 35**)

Acts 10:45
Jewish believers astonished that Gentiles were converted without first becoming Jewish
God moved mightily to show that the Church operated separate from Israel.

Acts 11:1, 18
Church in Jerusalem examines Gentiles being saved apart from becoming Israelites
Church recognizes that Gentiles are brought into the Church by God

Acts 13:44-46
Paul and Barnabas try to reach Israelites first.
They publicly turn to the Gentiles with the expansion of the Church.

Acts 15:1, 7-11
Some taught Israel and the Church are the same; no salvation (gospel) without the law (Israel).
Church council rejected this and stated the uniqueness of the Church.

Acts 18:6
Paul again turns from Jews to Gentiles.
The contrast of Israel (revived) and Church (Gentiles mostly) is emphasized.

Acts 28:25-29
Change from Israel to Church was prophesied by Isaiah.
The gradual change in Acts is clarified at the end of the book.

-SALVATION AND CIRCUMCISION

John 4:22
Jesus was witnessing to a Samaritan (non-Israelite)
At this point salvation was of the Jews.

Gal. 3:23-29
No longer is salvation of the Jews.
The Church is far more inclusive (**28**).
Through Christ we receive the benefits of Abraham.

Col. 2:9-13

Through Christ we have spiritual circumcision in contrast to Israel's physical.

This removes "**the body of the sins of the flesh**" (**11**) so that we can live obediently.

THREE SEPARATE JUDGMENTS

-JUDGMENT SEAT OF CHRIST

Rom. 14:10-12 – must give an account

II Cor. 5:9-11 – works judged, both good and bad

I Cor. 3:12-17 – only useful works survive

- JUDGMENT OF THE NATIONS

Matt. 25:32-46

Nations are judged (**32**)
Reward is to enter the Kingdom (**34**)
Decision based on works – what was done with God's people
Doom is everlasting fire based on not helping God's people

-GREAT WHITE THRONE OF JUDGMENT

Rev. 20:11-15

Lost are judged
Works are basis of judgment – out of books
Different time, passage, setting, and process than for the saved
Two Resurrections

John 5:28, 29

Two classifications of people
Two different resurrections

II Tim. 4:1

Two groups to be judged – the quick and the dead
Two times of resurrection for judgment – appearing and Kingdom

Rev. 20:4-6

One group lives after resurrection for 1000 years (**4**)
This is the first resurrection (**5**)
Second group is dead during the 1000 years

> Those of the first resurrection will not experience the second death (**14**)

THE CHURCH IN REVELATION

Rev. 1:11, 12, 20 – Church is on earth

Rev. 2:1, 7, 8, 11, 12, 17, 18, 23, 29 – Church is on earth

Rev. 3:1, 6, 7, 13, 14, 22 – Church is on earth

Rev. 22:16 – Next and last mention of Church
> Seen only in Heaven or with Christ after Rev. 4:1 (I Thess. 4:17b)
> Rev. 1:3; 19:7-10, 11-16; 20:6, 9.
> Purpose of the Tribulation

Rev. 6:10, 11
> Judgment and vengeance
> Heb. 10:30

Rev. 6:17
> Wrath poured out

I Thess. 5:9

Rev. 9:20-21

OFFER REPENTANCE AGAIN

Rev. 14:7; 16:9-11

Rev. 12:17
> Satan's greatest attack on the Jews

Rev.17:1
> Judgment on the "*One World Church*"

Rev. 18:1, 2, 5-8, 20, 24

Rev. 19:21-20:3
> Preparation for the Millennium

Rev. 11:2, 3
> Fulfillment of Israel's last 7-years (one week)
> Rev. 12:6, 14; 13:5; Rom. 11:13-28

CHAPTER 11
SPIRITUAL GIFTS

I Cor. 12:1

There are such things as spiritual gifts (perhaps as many as 21 named in the Bible).

God does not want Christians ignorant in this area.

I Cor. 12:2, 3

Gentiles are more likely to be led into idolatry on this subject.

There is a false leading in this area that carries people away from the truth.

The person, name, and position of Christ must remain central in our evaluation of wrong movements of our day. The issue is not the speech or speaker that sways, but Jesus and what is said of Him. There are three options:

Speaking wrongly about the Jesus of the Bible.

Speaking correctly about the Jesus of the Bible.

Avoiding the Jesus of the Bible.

ONLY THOSE WHO SPEAK CORRECTLY OF JESUS ARE DOING SO BY THE HOLY GHOST.

I Cor. 12:4-6

One of the keys to the gifts from the Holy Ghost is that there is great variety.

Variety of gifts (perhaps up to 21).

Each gift with differences of administrations.

Each administration with diversities of operations.

If there were 20 gifts, each with 20 administrations, and each of those with 20 operations, then we would have 8,000 possibilities. If we decrease the gifts but increase administrations and operations, the number could greatly increase. The likelihood of two similar gifted people being in the same church is most unlikely.

I Cor. 12:7

This may be the best Biblical definition of a spiritual gift.

Gifts are how the Spirit <u>manifests</u> Himself to others through us.

Gifts are given to <u>all</u> the saved.

We are expected to profit, or expand or develop on our gifts. Consider Christ's teaching on such (**Matt. 25:14-30; Luke 19:11-26**).

This is something different from talents. Talents are abilities we are born with and which can be developed.

These gifts are given; not earned, deserved, begged, etc.

I Cor. 12:11, 18

Gifts are given by the third member of the triune Godhead, the Holy Ghost (**vs. 11**).

They are given according to the will of the Spirit – not the will of man (**vs. 11**).

The Holy Spirit gives several (severally) gifts to every believer, not just one. We should know our gifts or areas and ways the Holy Spirit works through us. We certainly should not be ignorant of how we are best used by God (**vs. 11, 1**).

This is the basis of our functioning in the body of Christ (**vs. 18**).

I Cor. 12:8-10

The gifts are scattered among different believers.

No one gift is given to all Christians.

I Cor. 12:28

God clearly declares the order, ranking, rating, or valuing of the gifts.

"First" is the first and highest.

"Secondarily" is the second level and next highest.

"Thirdly" is the third level. If these three are a grouping as **Eph. 4** suggests, they are laid out carefully in order of importance.

"After that" drops to another level of operation.

"Then" drops to the lowest level with priority given in order.

I Cor. 13:1-3

Gifts without charity (practical love) are worthless.

We profit (**12:7**) nothing and are nothing in the Kingdom without love.

I Cor. 12:29-30

Not all gifts are given to any one person.

Thus we need others to minister to us and others need us to minister to them.

CHAPTER 11: SPIRITUAL GIFTS

I Pet. 4:10, 11
We are to be stewards of our gift(s). (**"It is** required in stewards, that a man be found faithful" (I Cor. 4:2).
Speaking gifts to be exercised with authority.
Ministry gifts to be exercised to the full **"ability which God giveth"**.
All exercise of gifts is for God's glory and never man's.

I Cor. 12:31
Some gifts are better than others, and some are called "*best*".
We are not to covet the lesser gifts but rather the "*best*" gifts.
There is something even better than coveting gifts – a "*way*" of life or behavior tied to our gifts...love.

I Cor. 13:4-7
Gifts exercised without love are worthless.
Gifts exercised with love will have definite evidences.

long suffering	- kind
no envy	- no boasting (vaunting)
no pride	- well behaved
unselfish	- not easily provoked
thinketh no evil	- not happy over sin
rejoices in truth	- carries burdens
full of faith	- full of hope
endures time and trials	

Eph. 4:7-16
The ascended Lord has given gifted people to the Church.
Ministers are gifts from God of gifted people and to be recognized as such.
Five areas are mentioned in **verse 11**.
These are given to accomplish ministries in the Church as stated in **verses 12-16**.
The evidence of gifted ministers being gifted of God is what is produced in the Church.
The issue is quality rated rather than quantity rated.
Their ministry perfects or makes complete (well rounded) saints who then minister to the world and edify one another (the body of Christ).
These men are needed until:
"we all come to the unity of the faith"

we all come to a full knowledge of Jesus as the Son of God.
we all come to mature, complete, well rounded (perfect) lives.
we all come to measure up to full conformity with Jesus (in all His fullness).
These ministers are needed that:
all grow up and are no longer spiritual children
there be stability of doctrine
believers not be carried away, fooled, or deceived; but rather consistent.
These ministers are needed and will produce Christians:
speaking the truth in love
growing up
the Church working together
the Church growing and ministering to herself

Ex. 35:30-35

The Holy Spirit gifts some men to produce items physically of beauty to assist in worship.
They were also gifted to teach each other these skills. Here is a case of skills coming from God and the ability to pass them on to others!

WRONG ATTITUDES ABOUT SPIRITUAL GIFTS

Spiritual gifts make us spiritual

I Cor. 1:7

The Church of Corinth was second to none in the matter of gifts.
They were also in one of the poorest conditions of any Church named in the New Testament (**1:11; 3:3; 4:18; 5:1; 6:1; 8:4, 9, 12; 11:18, 19, 21; 16:22**).
Their sins did not hinder their gifting even as their gifting was no evidence of spirituality.
I only need to minister in the areas of my gift(s).

II Tim. 4:5

Timothy was a much gifted man (**I Tim. 1:18; 4:14; II Tim. 1:6**).
He was commanded to operate as an evangelist – "***do the work of***" – even though he was not gifted to "***be an evangelist***".

GIFTS ARE FOR PERSONAL USE AND ENJOYMENT.

I Cor. 14:12

Emphasis is not on gifts but others.

CHAPTER 11: SPIRITUAL GIFTS

Our value is determined by what we do for others, especially the Church.
Spiritual gifts replace the authority of God's Word.

I Cor. 14:37, 38

The Word of God is the sole source of God's commands.
Gifts are never to replace or supercede it.
Denial of Scriptural authority over gifts is ignorance.

GIFTS AND THE BODY OF CHRIST

Rom. 12:4-6

Believers each have different offices and functions.
Together we make one body.
Gifts are given for functioning in the body.

I Cor. 12:11-18

Holy Spirit distributes the gifts according to the needs of the body.
Our difference is our basis of helping others.
Other's difference is their basis of helping us.

I Cor. 12:19-24

If we were alike, we would not be a body.
We need each other with our differences of gifts.
The more feeble (seemingly) are the most needed.
Those less honored are the most essential.

I Cor. 12:25-28

This stops divisions.
This promotes caring for each other.
This creates unity, empathy, and appreciation.

I Cor. 12:7-11

The division of the gifts is for the good of the body.
The gift(s) of the individual are not their choice but the Holy Spirit's according to the need as they are (not necessarily as we see them).

SPECIFIC GIFTS GIVEN

WORD OF WISDOM

I Cor. 12:8

— The ability to have insight into people and situations that is not obvious to the average person; combined with an understanding of what to do and how to do it.

Gen. 41:46, 37-39

Ex. 36:1, 2

Deut. 34:9

I Kings 3:5-12, 28

Prov. 2:6, 7

II Pet. 3:15, 16

James 3:13-18, 1:5

WORD OF KNOWLEDGE

I Cor. 12:8

— The ability to understand things which others do not know and cannot comprehend on their own.

I Cor. 13:2

      13:8-10

2:9-14

8:1

II Cor. 12:7

Matt. 16:13-17

Dan. 1:17, 20

2:19-23

Luke 8:10

II Tim. 2:7

FAITH

I Cor. 12:9

Eph. 2:8-10

Rom. 1:17

I Cor. 13:2

— The ability to see what others cannot see and to trust God in difficult situations.

— The ability to see beyond the obstacles – to know the God who delights in the impossible.

Heb. 11:8-19

Rom. 4:18-21

Acts 6:5, 8
     7:54-60

Mark 4:35-41

Heb. 11:1
     11:33
     11:1-40

GIFTS OF HEALING (S)

I Cor. 12:9
     12:28
     12:30

— The ability to cause a complete and instantaneous physical healing by direct command and/or touch.

Matt. 8:8, 13

Mark 5:28, 29

Mark 16:18

Luke 9:1-6

Acts 3:1-8
     5:15, 16
     9:41, 42

28:8, 9

James 5:14-20

WORKING OF MIRACLES

I Cor. 12:10

    12:28

    12:29

--- The ability to perform supernatural acts that clearly demonstrate that God's power is greater than that of Satan. Most commonly seen today in the casting out of demons.

Luke 4:33-36

    9:1

Mark 16:15-18

Acts 6:8

    8:5-8

    19:11, 12

PROPHECY (PROPHETS)

I Cor. 12:10

    This is a gift and prophets are gifted in this area (great shortage).
    The ministry is primarily in the reviving of believers.

Eph. 4:7-11

    Jesus gives prophets to men, to the Church.
    Probably the most rejected of all ministers (ex. Elijah, Jeremiah, Jonah, John the Baptist, etc.).

I Cor. 12:28, 29

    An obvious area of ministry.
    Ranked as second highest in this grouping.

Psm. 105:15

    Special warning given for treatment of prophets.

Ministry deals particularly with exposing sin and demanding repentance (ex. Nathan, Elijah, Isaiah, Jonah, John the Baptist).

Eph. 2:19-22
Apostles and Prophets make up the <u>foundation</u> of the Church.
Prophets call people back to Jesus the Chief Cornerstone.

Eph. 3:5
Receive special revelation (not inspiration) to give to others.
Revelation has to do with the local Church functioning in victory and to God's glory.

FUNCTION

Deut. 18:18, 19
Jesus the great example.
Speak under the control of God.
To speak God's Word (revelation) as already received by them.

II Kings 17:13
Ministry is to call for turning back to God from sin.
Their ministry will match with other prophets of God.
Consider II Chron. 24:19; Jer. 23:21, 22; 35:15

Acts 13:1
Has a ministry **in** the local Church.
Co-operates with other ministers as a partner.

Acts 15:32-33
Confirms believers in the faith.

I Cor. 14:3
To edify, exhort, and comfort.

Num. 11:25-29
Must know of Spirit's anointing.

II Pet. 1:20, 21
Must be holy men.
Must speak only at the moving of the Holy Ghost.

I Cor. 14:24, 25
Exposes sin in the lost also.
Produces worship to God by others.

ADDITIONAL NOTES
Amos 3:7
> Secrets revealed

Jer. 27:18
> Prayer

Jer. 25:4, 5
> Turn

I Sam. 3:19, 20
> Let none of their words fall.

<u>Much</u> warning of false prophets in the N.T. and O.T. and of those who claim the office falsely and/or counterfeit it.

DISCERNING OF SPIRITS

— Recognition of source behind words, action, and/or individuals:
> God's Holy Spirit
> Satan's demon spirits
> Man's human spirit

— Different from opinion, guess, experience, or testing.

I Cor. 12:10
> A gift.

I John 4:1-6
> Using scripture to test.
> All saints should test but discerning goes beyond this.

Acts 16:16-18
> Appearance of a helper to the Gospel.
> Discernment revealed it was demonically energized.

Matt. 16:22, 23
> Peter had just made a great pronouncement of God revealed truth (**vss. 16, 17**).
> Now he speaks in defense of Jesus.
> Discernment uncovers the second statement to be given by Satan thru Peter.

CHAPTER 11: SPIRITUAL GIFTS

I Cor. 14:29
> Often given to discern whether prophets are speaking by God's direction or not.

I Cor. 6:1-8
> Helps sort out difficult problems between believers in the Church.
> May be given to those least esteemed in the Church.
> & 9) Speaking in Tongues and Interpretation of Tongues

These seem to be the most abused gifts, practiced in the most unbiblical fashion, and most counterfeited of all gifts.

ON SPEAKING IN TONGUES

The following material is not to be taken as either a recommendation or a condemnation of speaking in tongues (**I Cor. 14:39b**). The purpose is simple. If speaking in tongues is of God, then it <u>must</u> conform to God's rules. However, conforming to these rules does not guarantee that it is of God. <u>If speaking in tongues breaks the rules of God, then it is not of God</u>. If it keeps the rules, then we should try the spirit to see if it is the <u>Holy Spirit</u> (**I John 4:1-4**).

<u>If you are spiritual</u>, you will accept the authority of God's Word on this subject of His rules on the tongues issue (**I Cor. 14:37**). <u>If you desire to be ignorant</u> in this area, you will succeed! (**I Cor. 14:38**).

The term "tongues" will be used to refer <u>only</u> to that which is a true gift of the Holy Spirit. In that <u>tongues are being counterfeited by demons and/or the flesh,</u> these rules apply only to that which is of God.

RULES ON TONGUES SPEAKING

> Do not covet or seek to speak in tongues (**I Cor. 12:31a, 28**)
> Tongues are worthless if you don't have true love (**I Cor. 13:1**).
> True tongues will not cause divisions in the Church, but rather will establish unity (**I Cor. 12:25**) ... There will be no confusion caused by the tongues, but the result will be peace (**I Cor.**

14:33) ... All things, tongues included, are to be done decently and in order (**I Cor. 14:40**).

Not all saved will be able to speak in tongues (**I Cor. 12:30, 10, 11**).

Tongues are the least important and least valuable of all gifts (**I Cor. 12:28, 30**), and therefore would not usurp the most important GIFTS OF THE HOLY SPIRIT.

Five (5) words spoken with understanding are more important than 10,000 words in an unknown tongue (**I Cor. 14:19**), and therefore tongues will not replace teaching and preaching.

Tongues are not to be used unless they edify others (**I Cor. 14:26, 23**).

There must be at least two, but no more than three speaking when the tongues are used (**I Cor. 14:27**).

These two or three are to take turns (**I Cor. 14:27**).

There is to be one interpreter – no more, no less (**I Cor. 14:27**).

If there is no interpreter, there is to be no speaking (**I Cor. 14:28**).

Women are not permitted to speak (either in tongues or interpreting) (**I Cor. 14:34**).

APOSTLES

I Cor. 12:28, 29
There is such a gift

Eph. 4:7-11
Those who have the gift and exercise it are given to men and the Church.

— APOSTLE COMES FROM A GREEK WORD.

Missionary comes from the Latin translation of that same word.

Apostle (Greek)= Missionary (Latin)= Sent One (English)

— THREE KINDS OR LEVELS OF APOSTLES

Heb. 3:1 - Jesus
Luke 22:14 - The twelve apostles
Acts 14:4, 14 - Paul and Barnabas (I Cor. 9:1, 2, 6)

Rom. 16:7 - **Andronicus and Junia**

CHAPTER 11: SPIRITUAL GIFTS

I Cor. 4:6, 9   **- Apollos and Sosthenes (1:1)**
- Timothy (:17)

Eph. 2:19, 20
Foundational to the Church.
Point people to Jesus.
Lay the foundation of the local Church.

Eph. 3:1-7
Have special understanding of a Biblical local Church.
God works through them in a special power and way in establishing Churches among the heathen.

FUNCTION

Acts 14:4
Separate out those who will respond to the Gospel.

Acts 14:21, 22
Preach the Gospel.
Instruct the converts.
Solidify the believers.
Prepare believers for persecution.

Acts 14:23-28
Ordain elders.
Work in starting several churches.
Report back to the Church who sent them.

CALLING

Gal. 1:1
Not chosen by man.
Selected by God.

Acts 13:1-4
First active and needed in the local Church.
Called by God.
Leaders of Church informed by God of the call.
Sent by the Church as well as by the Holy Spirit.

Rom. 15:20
Desiring to open new territory for Jesus.

EVANGELISTS

Eph. 4:7-11
God gifted men.
Given to Churches

I Cor. 12:28, 29
Not listed with some of the other areas of the ministry.
Not in list of "are all _____"?
Not set aside as area only for some to minister in.

Acts 21:8
Phillip is the only man clearly identified as "an evangelist".
His life and ministry should shed much light on a Biblical description of this position. (Differs from a commercialized professional Hollywood style of our day).
Examine Acts 6:3-7; 8:4-40.

II Tim. 4:5
Not all are gifted in evangelism.
All should do the work of an evangelist.

PASTORS

Eph. 4:7-11
God gifts men in this area.
God gives the gifted men to the Churches (**Jer. 3:15; 23:4**).

I Cor. 12:28, 29
Not listed with some areas of the ministry.
Clearly defined in Scriptures (see notes on Doctrine of the Church).

Acts 14:23
Elders were ordained in the Churches.
Titus 1:5-11 gives the qualifications of elders.
These are the same as for the Bishop **(vs. 7)**.
I Tim. 3:1-7 gives the qualifications of the Pastor.
A Church may have several elders but only one Pastor. All pastors are elders but not all elders serve as pastors.
The qualifications are high for the office is heavy and lesser qualified men will break under the load and hurt the Church.

Acts 20:28-32

Pastors (and elders) are to watch over the flock/church – protect, instruct, feed, oversee, and warn.

The health and safety of the local Church is in the hand of the pastor.

(John 10:10-15; I Pet. 5:1-4).

TEACHERS

I Cor. 12:28, 29

A highly esteemed gift.

Eph. 4:7-11

Gift given by God to men.
These gifted men are given to Churches.
They work very closely with Pastors.

Eph. 4:12-16

Their teaching lays the foundation for growth of the Church spiritually and numerically.

I Tim. 3:2

Pastors are to be gifted in this area also.

Titus 1:9-11

All elders are to have this gift.

Acts 13:1-4

This is one of the gifts exercised by the men in leadership at the Church in Antioch.

It was from this group that the first two missionaries were selected by God.

II Tim. 2:2

Teachers are to first learn and then teach others (**2:15**).
Their teaching is to be thorough enough that the learners become teachers of others, etc.

II Tim. 2:24-26

Teaching should be gentle and with patience.
Teachers must know how to meekly instruct those who oppose (them) and themselves with unrepented sin in their lives.

I Tim. 2:12
> Women are not to teach <u>over</u> a man – from a position of authority.
> Women are to act under authority and not usurp it.

Titus 2:3-5
> Women are to teach other women.
> There are some subjects only women should teach women.

GIFT OF HELPS
> Often overlooked and undervalued
> One of the most essential in the Church
> Absolute necessity for proper function of other gifts.

— The relieving of burdens and/or responsibilities of others by providing immediate support and/or help.
> See a need or opportunity and plunge in and do it.
> Willing to work in the background assisting others.

I Cor. 12:1, 7, 11, 18
  12:28

Ex. 18:22

Num. 11:14-17

Acts 20:35

SHOWING MERCY

Rom. 12:8

— The ability to have immediate compassion for those suffering physically, combined with great joy in meeting those needs.

Matt. 9:27
  15:22
  17:15
  20:30-34

Luke 10:30-37

17:13

Acts 9:39, 40

GIFTS OF "GIVING"

    All Christians are to give yet some are gifted in this area.

I Chron. 29:1-19

Rom. 12:3-8

John 12:2-8

II Cor. 8:1

        :2

        :3

        :4

        :5

        :6

        :7-8

        :9

        9:6-8

Phil. 4:15-19

EXHORTATION

    Closest to <u>Biblical</u> counseling (pastor, apostle).
    All Christians have some ability yet some are gifted in this area.

— To advise, counsel, encourage, persuade, caution, urge earnestly, comfort, or recommend.

    2 ideas
    One along side of
    Always from authority (Scriptures)

Rom. 12:8

    Gifted need to dwell on this ministry as teach and teaching.
    Will require much Bible study.

Acts 11:19-23
    Example of Barnabas.

Acts 14:21, 22
    Example of Paul and Barnabas.

Acts 15:31, 32
    Example of Silas and Jonas – resulted in establishing (confirming).

I Tim. 4:13
    Don't forget to minister in this area – give attention to it.

I Tim. 6:2
    Encourage to put facts into action – <u>employers</u>.

SUBJECTS ARE VARIED

Titus 1:9
    ** Always use God's Word – <u>correction</u>

II Thess. 3:12
    Put commands into action – <u>work and eating</u>

I Tim. 2:1
    Issue of <u>prayers, etc</u>.

I Pet. 5:1, 2
    Issue of <u>ministers</u>

MANNER OF EXHORTING

I Thess. 2:11
    As father to child.

I Thess. 5:14
    Patient toward all.

II Tim. 4:2
    With doctrine – suffering to do it.

Titus 2:15
    With authority and honor.
    Ruling

— To oversee, give leadership, be at the head.

Always with consideration of needs of others.
Always with an eye on goals.

Rom. 12:8
> Rule with diligence.

I Tim. 3:4, 5, 12
> Requirement for pastors/deacons.
> Picture – as a father
>   – as an elder (**I Tim. 5:17**)
> Test is seeing needs met in the lives of those you lead and proper goals accomplished.

I Thess. 5:12
> Over you

Heb. 13:7, 17, 24
> Rule over you.
> Follow/honor/judgment and accounting.
> Governments

— To administrate, give direction, translate goals into practice, make decisions on process, to organize.

I Cor. 12:28

Titus 1:5
> Titus an example.

II Tim. 2:2
> Timothy an example.
> Work out the details.

I Tim. 1:3
> Timothy
> Test is the smooth and efficient operation of work involving many details.
> Ministry

— To put into practice, implement, care for the details, serve.

Similar to Helps (helping others) but serving others may be doing it all yourself.
Pattern of Jesus ministering to us (term also refers to general of all gifts ministering).

Rom. 12:7
Stick with your work

Col. 1:7, 23, 25
Servant
Gospel
Church

II Tim. 1:16-18
To individual Christians.

Heb. 6:10
To the saints.

Acts 6:1-4
Needs of widows
Put out the Word to needs of people

Matt. 20:26-28
Humility
Example of Jesus

I Pet. 4:10, 11
As God makes us able

Philemon 13
To Paul in prison

II Cor. 11:15
Counterfeits

I Cor. 16:15
Addicted to the ministry.
Given over to sacrifice, suffering, loss, expense, - one factor in life.

HOSPITALITY

— Ability to entertain guests in your home with joy and show the goodness of Jesus.

Rom. 12:13, 9
    Without hypocrisy

I Pet. 4:9-11
    Without grudging

I Tim. 3:2
    Ministers are given to it

Titus 1:8
    Love hospitality

Heb. 13:2
    Towards strangers

Gen. 18:1-8
    Abraham an example

— Hospitality is a powerful tool of evangelism, fellowship, and strengthening.

ABOUT THE AUTHOR

J. PAUL RENO has been a pastor in Ohio and Maryland since 1968. During this time he has also been involved in church planting, training men for the ministry and speaking on mission fields in Europe, the Middle East, Africa, South America and Mexico. The church he presently pastors has just passed sending over three million dollars to missions. He continues to speak at various Bible conferences, camp meetings and local churches. He presently serves on the Board of Directors for the Conversion Center, which is headquartered in Hagerstown, Maryland. He has also written *To Fight or Not to Fight*, as well as over fifty pamphlets and booklets on salvation, the Christian life, Bible doctrine and the King James Version. His wife, Carolyn authored *Almost But Lost*, available as a free ebook download at

http://www.theoldpathspublications.com/Pages/Free.htm.

Paul is the father of five children, all of whom are active in the Lord's work with three serving presently as missionaries in Brazil.